# The Enemy
# Inside Your Mind

# The Enemy
# Inside Your Mind

*by*

*Bishop Paul S. Morton*

**THE ENEMY INSIDE YOUR MIND**

ISBN 1-880809-48-6

Printed in the United States of America

Copyright © 2005—by Bishop Paul S. Morton

Legacy Publishers International

1301 South Clinton Street

Denver, CO  80247

Phone: 303-283-7480  FAX: 303-283-7536

Library of Congress Cataloging-in-Publication Data
Pending

2 3 4 5 6 7 8 9 / 09 08 07 06 05

# Contents

*And ye shall know the truth, and the truth shall make you free.*

John 8:32

# Introduction

————⟫•⟨————

Most of us are aware of the existence of enemies in our lives, but many of us are only aware of external enemies, those that we can readily see. These, however, are not the most dangerous of our enemies. Our real enemies, those that seriously threaten our very existence and lessen the quality of our daily lives, are unseen and, therefore, often overlooked. These are the enemies that should have our attention, and the most serious of them is the enemy inside your mind, the enemy that works to convince you that his lies are actually truths.

It is this sowing of misconception, misunderstanding, and misinformation that often causes us to waste our God-given opportunities and resources and to take wrong turns in life, and it is perpetuated by him who is the avowed enemy of God, and thus the enemy of God's crowning creation—man. This enemy's goal is clear. Jesus said:

*The thief cometh not, but for to steal, and to kill, and to destroy.*

John 10:10

You are the target of Satan's ire. He wants to steal from you. He wants to pull you down. He wants to destroy you. And he won't be happy unless he can see you suffering in the flames of hell. This is a deadly serious matter.

Because we can see external enemies, we worry about them, and we make a conscious effort to defeat them. But because we cannot see the enemy inside our minds, we are often unconcerned about him and fail to put forth the necessary effort to keep him in check. Consequently, he overcomes us, and it happens far too often—even among professing Christians. This is a matter that merits our urgent attention. If we can learn to handle this enemy, we can handle all of the enemies that may come our way.

One example of the work of the enemy in your mind is his attempt to fill you with hate. As believers in Christ, it really doesn't matter when someone hates us. Such a person cannot stop our blessings. The danger arises when the enemy in our minds causes us to begin to hate those who hate us. That's when we start to lose God's blessing. As long as we refuse to allow the enemy who is operating in the minds of our detractors to operate in our minds as well, we can win every time. But once we allow him to operate in us, we lose. This is why it is so important that we learn to deal with the enemy of hate who is trying to enter our minds.

Other examples of this enemy's lies include his insistence that the circumstances of our birth should limit our possibilities in life, that because we have certain physical limitations, we can never go as far in life as others, and a whole myriad of other deceits and distortions. It's time to put these untruths to rest by employing the real truth. It's time to discover what is real and what is myth. The truth can bring you total release in every area of your life. So let us now use it to put to flight *The Enemy Inside Your Mind.*

*Bishop Paul S. Morton*

*New Orleans, Louisiana*

# CHAPTER 1

# Identifying and Confronting the Enemy Within

———✤———

*For we wrestle not against flesh and blood, but against principalities, against powers, against the rulers of the darkness of this world, against spiritual wickedness in high places.*

Ephesians 6:12

Each January, as we begin a new year, we often find that we are dealing with the very same problems we had the year before. We're still broke, we're still in pain, and this same cycle seems to continue year after year. Why is it that so many of us seem to be caught in a cycle of defeat? It's because there is an enemy hindering our progress, and we haven't known who or where that enemy is and how to go about defeating him.

At times, we have thought we finally knew who our real enemy was, and we expected a breakthrough, only to find that we were again mistaken and nothing really changed. Many of our setbacks in life are due to the fact that we have difficulty identifying our real enemy.

We are quick to blame other people, our job, our circumstances, or our environment. "Surely *this* must be the reason my life is what it is," we think. But these are only external factors, and I must declare once more that we are looking at the wrong enemy. The Scriptures tell us that we are not wrestling with externals, but with an internal force.

This term *"flesh and blood"* that Paul used in Ephesians 6:12 refers to people, and Paul said that *"we wrestle not"* with them. Well, then, if people are not the problem, what is? Our problem, Paul went on to say, is *"principalities"* ... *"powers"* ... *"rulers of the darkness of this world"* ... *"spiritual wickedness in high places."* And why? Because these *"principalities"* and *"powers"* war against our minds. *"The rulers of the darkness of this world"* and *"spiritual wickedness in high places"* war against our minds.

### Your Real Enemy

Stop wrestling with people. They're not your problem. Learn who your real enemy is. Satan's legions are arrayed against your mind. Start taking authority over them, or they will hinder your progress continually. Your greatest enemy is even now at work inside your mind.

When the enemy attacks our minds, his desire is to build a stronghold there. The thoughts he brings to you are not just random ones. He has a well-intentioned plan, and he is carrying it out with precision. In the process, he is setting you up step by step for a fall. He wants to take you out, and he will stop at nothing to accomplish it.

The greatest danger to us is not to be found in the thoughts that we recognize as evil. Those are easy to overcome. The gravest danger to our souls comes from the wrong thoughts that have been harbored for so long that they have now become somehow acceptable.

For example, cursing has become such a part of our modern life that many people have come to accept it as "normal" and even "to be expected." This is a very dangerous thought pattern. Some people curse and don't even know they're cursing. The devil loves that. He delights in embedding things so deeply within our thinking that we cannot prevent them from bubbling to the surface, and what's worse, we're not alarmed when they do appear.

Then, when things don't go right for us, we're quick to blame our parents, our spouses, or our friends and associates, and we fail to realize that evil is lurking within *us*. It is hidden sin within us that brings victory to Satan every time. Your greatest battle in life is with your own mind.

### Jesus' Greatest Battle Was with His Mind

Jesus had to face every temptation we face, and His greatest battle was with His mind. Matthew wrote of our Lord's temptation:

3

*Then was Jesus led up of the Spirit into the wilderness to be tempted of the devil.*

Matthew 4:1

When I began to understand more fully Jesus' wilderness experience, it opened my mind to the reality of how badly the enemy wants to get inside of our minds. For many years, I thought of His temptation in connection with a certain geographical location, but as I began to examine more closely the biblical account, I realized that what Jesus experienced had nothing to do with where the events took place. It had everything to do with His mind.

While He was here on the earth, Jesus was in a human body, and because He was in a human body, He followed the natural laws that govern human beings. He didn't magically hop from one place to another, and He didn't twitch His nose like Samantha on the television series "Bewitched" and appear and disappear at will. When He was tempted, therefore, and the temptation included taking Him to *"the holy city,"* He had not gone there physically, but in His mind:

*Then the devil taketh him up into the holy city, and setteth him on a pinnacle of the temple.*

Matthew 4:5

How could the devil have taken Jesus into the Holy City and sat Him on the pinnacle of the temple when there was no temple in the wilderness, and they were far from the Holy City at that moment? He must have drawn the picture in Jesus' mind. Satan has that power.

Jesus was taken to the Holy City, He was sat upon the pinnacle of the temple, and there Satan taunted Him. If

He was the Son of God, He should be able to cast himself off of that highest point of the temple, and no harm would come to Him. As if to justify what he was suggesting, the devil quoted from Psalm 91:

*For he shall give his angels charge over thee, to keep thee in all thy ways. They shall bear thee up in their hands, lest thou dash thy foot against a stone.*

Psalm 91:11-12

Jesus was not caught off guard by this tactic. He recognized it for what it was and refused the enemy's offer, opposing Him with the Word of God quoted in its pure simplicity and truthfulness:

*Jesus said unto him, It is written again, Thou shalt not tempt the Lord thy God.*

Matthew 4:7

Our Lord knew what to answer when He was tempted, and we need to know what to answer when we're tempted too. We must learn to respond with power to this enemy who attacks our minds in an attempt to control us.

The devil wasn't finished with Jesus:

*Again, the devil taketh him up into an exceeding high mountain, and sheweth him all the kingdoms of the world, and the glory of them.*

Matthew 4:8

How high must that mountain have been for Jesus to be able to see so much from that place? In reality, Jesus was in an area where no mountain was extremely high,

5

and He could not have seen all the kingdoms of the world from any of the local mountains. Therefore, all that He was now seeing had to have been presented to Him in His mind.

*By rejecting Satan's lies and dwelling on God's truths, we can actually renew our minds.*

———

"I can give you all the kingdoms of the world," Satan was saying to Jesus. As usual, it was all lies, and Satan was only trying to confuse Jesus in an effort to control Him.

But, again, Jesus was not about to be controlled by this. He only allowed the truth of God's Word to control His reality, and now He deferred to it yet again:

> *Then saith Jesus unto him, Get thee hence, Satan: for it is written, Thou shalt worship the Lord thy God, and him only shalt thou serve.*
>
> Matthew 4:10

What will define your reality? Satan's lies and the beautiful pictures he paints in your mind? Or the truth of God's unchanging Word? By rejecting Satan's lies and dwelling on God's truths, we can actually renew our minds.

### A Renewed Mind

God is able to renew our minds, and He can do that regardless of what state they're currently in. If negative thinking has been a way of life for you, you can be transformed by the time you finish reading this book. It requires only that you properly identify your real enemy and his tactics and that you seek God for His help to overcome.

Once you have identified the enemy in your mind, the devil will no longer be able to bother you the way he has in the past. And, since you now know that the enemy is not another person, you can better channel your energies.

You must determine that Satan will no longer be able to get to your mind through what other people say or do to you. They may roll their eyes at you, curse you out, and talk about you like a dog, but still you must refuse to allow them to get inside your mind. When you know what's behind their actions and their words, you'll no longer allow these kinds of things to move you. This is just a trick of the enemy, who is even now trying to control your reality.

Satan wants you to become discouraged by what other people think about you. When sickness attacks your body, he wants you to believe that the pain you're experiencing is more powerful than the healing that God can bring you. He wants you to think that the troubles you're currently experiencing are bigger than the troubles others are suffering and that nothing can overcome them. Just the opposite is true. Paul wrote:

> *Now unto him that is able to do exceeding abundantly above all that we ask or think, according to the power that worketh in us, unto him be glory in the church by Christ Jesus throughout all ages, world without end. Amen.*
>
> Ephesians 3:20-21

If I can trust God, nothing is impossible to me. So I refuse to allow the devil to work inside my mind and to thus limit my reality.

### The Enemy Is Looking for a Dry Place

When looking for someone vulnerable to attack, the enemy searches for *"dry places"*:

> *When the unclean spirit is gone out of a man, he walketh through dry places, seeking rest, and findeth none.*
>
> Matthew 12:43

What does this mean, that the devil is looking for *"dry places"*? It means that he's looking for people who are depressed. He has sent out his imps—demons, or unclean spirits—to look for those who are discouraged and feel like there's no hope and no way out for them. They've been going through such rough places in life that they've reached the conclusion that there's no use trying anymore. They're convinced that they will never achieve anything in life, and that things will never change for the better for them. These are prime targets for Satan's deceptive work.

Satan is even looking for church folk. He sends his emissaries to look for those who go to church because they feel obligated to go, but who don't really expect anything in their lives to change. They are weakened, and when demons find such a one, their antenna goes up. "I've found a dry place," they say gleefully, and then they immediately set out to attack the minds of those weakened ones they find.

A demon fights hard to get inside the minds of wanderers because they know that there they can find fertile ground. Demons hate confusion and love to find places where they no longer have to struggle. They can rest.

And what is *"rest"* to a demon? Their idea of rest is to be in an environment they're accustomed to and comfortable with. When our thought lives are filled with unbelief, that makes the devil and his legions feel right at home. When we're not bothered by their presence, that delights them. They even feel comfortable with those who shout on Sunday, just as long as they're willing to live for the devil the rest of the week.

Our enemy likes rest. He doesn't like it when we say to him, "I bind you in the name of Jesus and command you to go." He doesn't want to have to struggle, so he searches for a place that is compatible with his temperament, where he can live in peace.

The devil loves to live with people who don't believe what the Bible says and who settle for the conflicting report of some "specialist." He uses such reports to gain control over us. He reminds us of the fact that a parent or grandparent died with the same disease and encourages us to accept a doctor's diagnosis.

### Overcoming the Thoughts That Keep Us Bound

Even though we find great comfort in the fact that we are Christians, just being a Christian does not in any way make us immune to Satan's attacks. Even within Christians, there is a war raging. Paul, one of the greatest Christians of all times, wrote:

*I find then a law, that, when I would do good, evil is present with me. For I delight in the law of God after the inward man: but I see another law in my members, warring against the law of my mind,*

9

*and bringing me into captivity to the law of sin
which is in my members.*

Romans 7:21-23

It is rare to find a Christian who has not been limited at some point by negative thinking. Christians harbor thoughts of unbelief. We're sometimes lukewarm in our love for the Lord, and we sometimes only speak to people and act lovingly toward them because we know that others are watching us. That's not real love. Fear, pride, and unforgiveness may also be found in us. If we were to be honest with ourselves, we would have to admit being limited by one or more of these things at some point in our Christian lives. We might also have to admit to lust, greed, jealousy, or any combination of these three.

And why is it that good Christians sometimes fall into sin? It's because the devil is very good at his job, and he is constantly attacking our minds. His mission is well defined, and he is even now on the prowl to fulfill it.

Many, if not most, of us are being attacked by unbelief on any given day. Then we wonder why everybody else is being blessed, and we're being passed over. To get our share of the blessing, we must take authority over our own unbelief and tell the devil to get out of our minds. We must make a decision to stand on the truth of God's Word. We may not have what we want right now, but we must believe that it's on the way as we put our trust in God.

The devil thrives where unbelief is present, so he does everything he can to spread it. He loves it when fear clouds our thinking, and if he had his way, we would all walk around in fear constantly.

God's will for us is very different:

*For God hath not given us the spirit of fear; but of power, and of love, and of a sound mind.*

2 Timothy 1:7

If the devil can succeed in filling our minds with fear, we will be powerless against him. Reject his lies, and you can live in peace.

Some were so traumatized by the events of 9/11 that they will no longer board an airplane. They would rather take a bus or a train or even drive. Osama Bin Laden doesn't have to do anything else to them; he already has them defeated and living in constant fear.

> *If the devil can succeed in filling our minds with fear, we will be powerless against him.*

Fear will paralyze you, just as it did the American economy after that great disaster struck. The reason the economy was so slow to recover is that people were afraid of just what else the future might hold.

Our reaction to fear has sometimes nearly brought our airline industry to a grinding halt, while people who could barely walk were being searched and x-rayed to make sure they were not carrying bombs or weapons aboard. This is the sad extent to which fear has gripped this great country of ours.

The devil is a master at creating fear, but we can take authority over him in the name of Jesus and let him know that we refuse to be held hostage to his taunts. Since fear is not of God, we should not want it in our lives, and every believer must make a conscious effort to reject it.

### The Need to Overcome Unclean Habits

Another area where Satan seeks to control us is with unclean habits. He tries to trap us into committing the same sin over and over again until it actually becomes a habit for us. Such habits are often unbreakable without God's help. Our sinning over and over again in this way makes the enemy feel right at home. He loves it.

Once he has a person hooked on sinning, the devil can relax more and take it easy. With some people, he has to work constantly to keep them controlled, but that's not the case with those whose sin has become an unclean habit. He has them, so he can relax.

The devil doesn't even care if people like this go to church and participate in worship services—as long as others don't come to know that they're bound and try to set them free. He knows that he controls their lives the rest of the week, so he's satisfied.

### The Need to Overcome Any Negative Family Heritage

Another tactic the enemy uses is to play on any negative family heritage we might have. For instance, he's a master at playing the race card. Far too many people in this world can't seem to get ahead in life due to the color of their skin. But, of course, it's all in their minds.

That doesn't make it any less real. In their minds, the fact that they're black means that they have to step back and allow others to go ahead of them. This is sad because any person who allows this concept to remain imbedded in their thinking will never be able to move on to the next level in life, and their true destiny will elude them.

Why should any aspect of our family heritage be something that holds us back? It doesn't matter if your parents or grandparents were not successful in life. Let the curse stop with them; you be blessed.

We must stop allowing the devil to remind us of how bad the people in our family are or were. Stop worrying about their negative attitudes and their negative ways. Decide that you will be successful and set out to be just that. What they were or are should have nothing at all to do with your future. You're a child of God, and nothing can hold you back—unless you let it.

Let the devil know today that you're determined to make a difference in life and that you refuse to allow him to stop you—no matter what the color of your skin or the past history of your family. Get all of those negative concepts our of your mind once and for all.

### The Need to Overcome Pride and Arrogance

With some people, it's just the opposite. They're limited, or bound, because they can't get over their own goodness. They think they're better than everybody else and that they're always right. To hear them tell it, you would think that they were the one exception to the *"all have sinned"* truth. They're somehow blinded to their own shortcomings.

Some of us readily excuse ourselves because it's difficult for us to discern areas of weakness in our own lives. We justify our negative thoughts, not realizing that our attitudes or perceptions are wrong.

God knows our hearts, and one day we will stand before Him and be judged. What will His verdict be on that day? Will you allow untrue thoughts to bring you into bondage and keep you from God's very best?

What you imagine is not necessarily truth. Will you become like those of whom the apostle Paul wrote:

*Because that, when they knew God, they glorified him not as God, neither were thankful; but became vain in their imaginations, and their foolish heart was darkened.*

Romans 1:21

Take authority over your vain imaginations.

### The Process of Deliverance

The process of deliverance from wrong thinking is not always an easy one. Often it involves a season of inner conflict and turmoil. Seemingly, in order to be freed from vain imaginations and bad thinking, we must engage in some inner conflict.

Some believe that inner conflict and turmoil is not good, but in this case, it is. When we experience inner conflict in this context, it simply means that the demons attacking our minds can't rest because we're resisting them. Like Paul, we find that when we would do good, evil is present with us, so we must not rest, but keep fighting. Let the devil know that although he is still on his feet now, there's no way he will win this battle.

Sometimes we fail, and sometimes we fall, but whatever happens, don't become discouraged. And don't become concerned about the turmoil and the inner conflict. This time, it's a good sign. It signifies our desire to be free and let's Satan know that we're tired of him "messing" with our minds, tired of him bothering us, and we don't intend to stand for it any longer.

### You Must Become Sick and Tired of It

To be effective in this struggle, you have to be serious, and that means being sick and tired of what the devil has done to you in the past. This doesn't mean that you're sick of the people around you. Remember, the problem is you and your mind, not other people.

You must be sick of the devil playing with your mind all day and all night, sick of the thoughts that fill you with hatred and jealousy, and you must be so sick of it that you simply will not permit it to continue. Tell the devil that you refuse to let him torment you any longer. Take authority over him and over the thoughts he has implanted in your mind, and do it in the name of Jesus.

You have that power, and you must take that authority. No one else can do that for you. Resist the devil. Don't play with him, and don't let him play with you. Let him know that you want him out of your mind now and, furthermore, that you expect him never to return. Throw him out of your house, and tell him to never come back.

Will it work? Of course it will. If you resist the devil, he *will* flee. When you resist him, he will find no place of lodging in your mind.

He won't go quietly, for the devil hates it when we resist him. But ignore whatever he does, block him out, and refuse to let him back in.

### It's Your Time

More than likely, the enemy has been bothering your mind for years and you didn't know where this opposition was coming from. You may well have been blaming your defeat in life on somebody else, but now you know the truth. You can say, "Lord, since it's not other people, I'm determined to work on me and on my destructive thoughts."

Now that you know where the enemy is, you must develop the desire to take authority over him because this is your time to receive the blessings God has prepared for you. This is your time to be an overcomer. Resist the devil now, and he will flee.

"Once I have resisted the devil, what happens next?" you might ask. Well, as I said, when you resist the devil, he gets mad. He doesn't want you to make positive steps toward doing the right thing, and he will try any and every way he can to stop you.

I speak from experience. Many years ago, while I was on a trip out of town, I was walking out of my hotel room and down the hall one day when one of the hotel maids spotted me. She looked me up and down and then said, "Um, you look good."

"I'm a married man," I responded immediately, "I don't play that game. You've got the wrong person," and I turned and walked away.

As I did, she shouted angrily, "I didn't want a short man anyhow."

Our resistance makes the devil mad, so be prepared for this.

Don't be surprised when the devil attacks you after you've decided to tithe from your income. He'll torment your mind and tell you not to do it because it doesn't pay. "Besides, you don't earn enough to make ends meet the way it is," he'll say. He will tell you that you would be a fool to tithe, but if you know God's Word on the subject, you can defeat him. God said:

> *Will a man rob God? Yet ye have robbed me. But ye say, Wherein have we robbed thee? In tithes and offerings. Ye are cursed with a curse: for ye have robbed me, even this whole nation. Bring ye all the tithes into the storehouse, that there may be meat in mine house, and prove me now herewith, saith the Lord of hosts, if I will not open you the windows of heaven, and pour you out a blessing, that there shall not be room enough to receive it.*
>
> Malachi 3:8-10

Since you know God's faithfulness in this matter, you can put the enemy in his place. But, again, don't think that he will just stand back and take it. He will not back off. Instead, he will attack your finances. He will attack your home and your job.

*Know that as you obey God and resist the devil, you will win— no matter what the devil decides to do.*

———•———

You must be so serious about renewing your mind through God's truth and overcoming Satan's lies once and for all that you don't care if he does get mad. Know that as you obey God and resist the devil, you will win—no matter what the devil decides to do.

"Why is all of this necessary?" some might ask. It's because we can never get things straight around us until we have gotten things straight within us. And getting things straight within us begins with our thought life.

Our parents and grandparents were accustomed to saying, "Devil, we cast you out of our minds." They knew the importance of keeping the devil out, and we must do the same. Tell him right now, "I'm casting you out of my mind," and then follow through with your intent. Consistently reject his lies and live in the freedom that truth brings.

### Break that Cycle of Defeat Right Now

If you've found yourself going through the same cycle year after year, each January hoping that the coming year will be different, you need to get rid of the root of your problem. Deal with what's been going on in your mind by turning your mind over to Jesus. Then let God

18

transform you. Your thinking may have been wrong for twenty or thirty years already, but God can change you. And He can enable you to live differently through following the truth of God's Word.

From today forward, if you want to know what to think on any given subject, open your Bible and ask God to show you. He will reveal to you what He wants you to think, and as you think His thoughts, you will be blessed. Rebuke the devil and his bad thoughts, and refuse to let him destroy your life.

It's time to turn every thought over to the Lord, commit yourself to thinking as God thinks, treating your enemies as Jesus treated His enemies, and loving as He loved. When you do this, you cannot help but walk in victory. This doesn't mean that the enemy will become nonexistent, but the Lord, who is greater than the enemy, will now be directing your thoughts.

What are you waiting for? This is your day of deliverance. Whenever someone speaks deliverance into your life, something will always happen, and I want to do that for you right now:

*Be freed from the thoughts that have kept you bound, and be cleansed in your heart so that you can be blessed.*

If you're willing to let God do what He wants to do in your life, you can put to flight *The Enemy Inside Your Mind.*

# CHAPTER 2

# Keys to Overcoming the Enemy Inside Your Mind

————⟫•◦•⟪————

*(For the weapons of our warfare are not carnal, but mighty through God to the pulling down of strong holds;) casting down imaginations, and every high thing that exalteth itself against the knowledge of God, and bringeth into captivity every thought to the obedience of Christ.*

2 Corinthians 10:4-5

It is wrong for Christians to be bound by the lies of Satan, for our God has equipped us with weapons that can give us victory over him. Just as he works inside our minds, the weapons also work to defend us inside our minds. With the weapons God has given us, we can cast down *"imaginations"* and bring *"into captivity every thought"* that is not in keeping with His will for our lives.

Our weapons are *"mighty"* and will enable us to *"pull down"* any *"strongholds"* the enemy has set up in our thinking. So what are we waiting for? It's time for us to use our God-given weapons and to tear down every stronghold of the enemy.

The *New International Version* of the Bible says it this way:

> *We demolish arguments and every pretension that sets itself up against the knowledge of God, and we take captive every thought to make it obedient to Christ.*
>
> 2 Corinthians 10:5, NIV

The power of God enables us to *"demolish"* such *"arguments"* and such *"pretentions"* and to bring them into submission to Christ and His Word.

The apostle Paul was the writer God used to give us these words. He was comparing himself with a warrior who was fiercely attacking some strongly protected place—a place known in ancient times as a "stronghold."

### What Are Strongholds? And How Are They Established in Your Mind?

*Webster's Revised Unabridged Dictionary* defines the word *stronghold* as: "a strongly fortified defensive structure." Picture in your mind such a stronghold and what might have been required for Paul to pull it down.

Over time, strong defenses had been set up, the place had been secured, and it was now well guarded. Paul must somehow overcome all the defenders of this stronghold and then remove it, if he was to go to the next level in his spiritual life. How could such a thing be accomplished?

In order to take control of this strongly protected place and remove it, Paul must first take captive one-by-one every wicked defender and somehow force their obedience to the Commander under whose authority he fought. That sounds like a very tall order, and yet Paul was not only able to do it himself; he went on to say that each of us can do the same thing through the weapons already at our disposal.

Strongholds form because the mind of man is a strange apparatus. It gets some thought in it—right or wrong, good or bad—and that thought becomes difficult to displace. It seems to get lodged there, stuck, if you will, refusing to budge. It's amazing how many sincere people are sincerely wrong, how many serious people are seriously in error. Oh, they think they're right, but they're not right. This is how prejudices develop.

The word *prejudice* simply means a prejudgment or, as *Miriam-Webster Online Dictionary* states, "a preconceived judgment or opinion, an adverse opinion or leaning formed without just grounds or before sufficient knowledge."

Most people are given to some type of prejudice. Without really knowing or understanding the details of a given situation, we prejudge it by what little we do know. Without really knowing or understanding a person, we prejudge them by their outward appearance or by some long-ago formed notion we hold about their particular race. But just because a situation looks a certain way doesn't mean that it *is* that way, and just because one member of a given race has proven bad doesn't mean that every member of that race is bad.

And then there's our imagination. The imagination of man easily runs wild. We imagine all sorts of things, and most of what we imagine proves to be unfounded. It's time to reject prejudices and to cast down imaginations, for they're our enemies and they hold us back from God's best for our lives.

In truth, the very mind of man is God's enemy:

*For to be carnally minded is death; but to be spiritually minded is life and peace. Because the carnal mind is enmity against God: for it is not subject to the law of God, neither indeed can be. So then they that are in the flesh cannot please God.*

Romans 8:6-8

Is it any wonder, then, that we must take control of our minds and be careful what finds lodging there? If God didn't speak a certain thing into your heart, stop entertaining it. To insist on believing the lies of the enemy or to constantly entertain the wild imaginations of your mind is an act of open rebellion against God.

Such rebellion is not to be found only in unbelievers. Many Christians are angry with God just because He wants them to behave themselves. They don't want Him meddling in their affairs and telling them what to do. There's little hope that such people will become strong

24

Christians anytime soon. But even strong Christians, to one degree or another, struggle with issues of the mind.

Just because we mature in Christ doesn't mean that the enemy will leave us alone. To the contrary. He goes after even the most powerful followers in Christ and is delighted if they fall. He is a threat to each of us, and each of us must face up to this fact personally. You have an enemy who wants very much to do you in. Learn to face him squarely and defend yourself.

*Just because we mature in Christ doesn't mean that the enemy will leave us alone.*

But stop trying to use carnal weapons in your fight. You're not fighting against Osama Bin Laden; your enemy is much more deadly than that elusive man. If you try to use your own weapons against *this* enemy, you will surely lose. The weapons we use to attack the prejudices and hostilities of our minds must have the power to convince and persuade.

### The Power to Convince and Persuade

Once your mind has come to believe a certain way, it's very difficult to convince it otherwise. Some of the prejudices we hold have been built up in us over many years. In some cases, we have even been taught these things all of our lives. This constant reinforcement of negative thoughts and stereotypes builds a stronghold in our minds, one that is not easily pulled down.

In a very real sense, we must learn to outthink our tapes if we are to outsmart the enemy. What do I mean by outthinking our tapes? Our "tapes" are myths that constantly play over and over within our minds, for we have come to accept them as truths about ourselves. They are thoughts that have been recorded within our minds through a lifetime. Although these thoughts are untrue, we believe them because we've heard them repeated so many times, and now our minds replay them over and over again.

It's our tapes that cause us to develop a negative self-image and, consequently, they cause us to walk in defeat. If we want victory, therefore, we must outthink these tapes that are present with us every single day.

You may be dealing with a tape that constantly tells you that you're nobody, and to overcome that, you must recognize what God's Word says about you:

*I will praise thee; for I am fearfully and wonderfully made: marvellous are thy works; and that my soul knoweth right well.*

Psalm 139:14

*For we are his workmanship, created in Christ Jesus unto good works, which God hath before ordained that we should walk in them.*

Ephesians 2:10

Based on these truths, learn to outthink your tapes and thus outsmart your enemy. If you cannot or will not do it, you will never walk in victory.

Our tapes work against us, for through them Satan works tirelessly to make us feel and act like failures. Once you get the belief in your mind that you're a failure, you'll start to feel like one, and then you'll start to act like one. Once you learn the truth, you can grow quickly and go to the next level by taking authority over the enemy and his lies.

### Fight Lies with Truth

Because a stronghold has been established in our minds, the weapon we use to dispel the error must be much stronger than the mind. The only weapon that can defeat lies is truth, and the only pure truth we have at our disposal is the Word of God. It *is* truth:

> *For the word of the Lord is right; and all his works are done in truth.*
>
> Psalm 33:4

> *Sanctify them through thy truth: thy word is truth.*
>
> John 17:17

After laying out the details of our battle with *"principalities and powers"* in Ephesians 6, Paul went on to say:

> *Wherefore take unto you the whole armour of God, that ye may be able to withstand in the evil day, and having done all, to stand.*
>
> Ephesians 6:13

It is critical that we learn how to take authority over the oppression and depression that Satan attempts to bring our way. Part of our ability to do that successfully comes with putting on the various elements of *"the armour of God."* The very first of those elements Paul mentioned is *"truth"*:

27

*Stand therefore, having your loins girt about with truth ... .*

Ephesians 6:14

Truth is our weapon of choice, and if, for some reason, I cannot put on truth, I will find myself constantly struggling with spiritual bondage.

Whatever the case, our mind is the battleground. It is there, in the mind, that the battle will either be won or lost. So winning or losing this battle depends on how well I learn to deal with truth.

*Truth, you will discover, is a tool that is greater than anything you may be called upon to face in life.*

———

Truth, you will discover, is a tool that is greater than anything you may be called upon to face in life. The minute you come to understand the power of God's Word in you, the devil will no longer be able to stop you. By using this weapon that can convince and persuade, you will prevail.

This weapon of truth is powerful:

*For the word of God is quick, and powerful, and sharper than any twoedged sword, piercing even to the dividing asunder of soul and spirit, and of the joints and marrow, and is a discerner of the thoughts and intents of the heart.*

Hebrews 4:12

When you become sick and your doctor says that you have a terminal illness, you can still believe for healing because you have the declaration of God's Word:

*But he was wounded for our transgressions, he was bruised for our iniquities: the chastisement of our peace was upon him; and with his stripes we are healed.*

Isaiah 53:5

With God's Word to back you up, you can thank your doctor for his report and still know that God will make you whole and cause you to live. Your weapons are not carnal, and you have found something that can convince and persuade your mind that what God says can be done and will be done. Truth wins out over lies every time.

The war of the mind is not one that can be won with winning manners or eloquent words. Applying philosophy will not help you here. You need something much more powerful this time. Only spiritual weapons will do, and only the truth of God can prevail over all of Satan's lies.

No matter how angry I become with someone, taking out a gun and shooting them would resolve nothing. Instead, I must use the spiritual weapons at my disposal.

Satan wants to destroy us any way he can, and he will use every tactic he can. But if we will use the weapons God has given us, we can defeat the devil every time. Pull down those strongholds! Cast down those imaginations! And bring into captivity every thought to the obedience of Christ! You can do it through the power given to you by almighty God.

But don't expect this fight to be an easy one. When you start bringing thoughts into captivity, Satan becomes very agitated. Some people roll their eyes wildly at their preacher when he tries to help them bring their minds into obedience to God through truth. He's only doing that because he loves them and wants them to have victory, but they resent it. This indicates that their mind is dangerously set, and they need to be delivered from terrible lies.

### The Power of Thought—the Distinctive Mark of Man

Thought is the distinctive mark that sets man apart from all the rest of the animal kingdom. On earth, there's nothing great but man. In man, there's nothing great but the mind. And the great function of the mind is to think. This ability to think, or reason, is man's greatest distinction. Other creatures may be able to think to some limited extent, but none of them is distinguished by their thoughts.

A man without thought is a man destitute of power. It doesn't matter how nicely he might dress, if he doesn't have a mind, nobody will want to be bothered with him. Some women are attracted to a man who has a nice automobile, but if they learn that he has no mind, they quickly come to the conclusion, "You can keep your car. You're not the man for me."

Because it is the mind that distinguishes man from every other creature, it is in the mind that Satan attacks us. This is the real battleground of life.

Think about the power of the mind. By the exercise of thought, we're able to transfer that which is without and bring it within us. In other words, we can actually carry the world in our minds. For instance, I don't have to be in Hawaii to know how it feels to be there. I can see the beach in my mind, and I don't have to be physically present to appreciate it.

Through the power of thought, we not only can recall the past; we can actually relive it. Many actually choose to live in the past because they prefer it. They're out there somewhere enjoying what they experienced many years ago. The mind is just that powerful, and that's why the enemy delights in setting up strongholds within it.

Through the power of thought, we can anticipate the future and actually inhabit it. I might not have a new home at this minute, but I can visualize one in my mind and start to enjoy it before it becomes reality. It is fairly common knowledge these days that if we can visualize some goal, we can attain that goal.

The mind is an awesome thing. Through it, we can walk in the invisible. Through the power of thought, we can dwell in a world that transcends the senses. Anything and everything that we cannot currently see with our eyes, smell with our nose, or hear with our ears can be known and appreciated if it's in our minds.

How powerful the mind is! And how careful we must be that it does not run away with us!

A man actually is what he thinks:

*For as he thinketh in his heart, so is he.*

Proverbs 23:7

In this way, the mind can either work for you are against you. If you can learn to think right, then blessings are in store for you, but if you cannot learn to think right, the enemy will take over your mind and abort your destiny.

Bad thoughts can become silent killers, and nothing is more dangerous. Cast them down without delay.

Command every silent killer to stop hindering your destiny. You are a child of God, and the devil has no right to get inside of your mind and take it over. Take authority over him today and cast him out. Dispel him with truth.

### The Rule of Exclusion

If you are to walk in your destiny, you must take authority over your thoughts and not allow destructive thoughts to control your actions. Allow me to give you three practical rules that will help you to control your thought life. The first one is called the rule of exclusion.

You may ask, "What do I need to exclude?" You must exclude all negative and adverse thoughts from your mind. Stop admitting negative thoughts into your mind, and stop nurturing them once they get there. In order to accomplish this, you will have to eliminate the evil influences that give birth to them in the first place.

A great artist once said that he did not allow himself to look at a bad painting because he found that if he did, it had a sinister effect upon his work for days afterward. Every time he tried to paint, he could still see that bad picture in his mind. And a painter paints what's in his mind.

The devil wants to put a bad picture in your mind, and then he wants you to look at that bad picture over and over again day and night until it consumes you. Satan knows that if he can get such a negative picture into your mind and get you focused on it, he can gain authority over you and cause you to go astray.

Learn to boycott every bad thought. Reject it and refuse to have anything to do with it. If you happen to run into a bad thought, turn away from it as fast as you can, and forget it just as fast as you can. If you insist on holding on to a bad thought, that simple thought can cause you to miss your destiny.

Tell every negative thought to get out of your mind. This is the rule of exclusion.

## The Rule of Attention

The second rule that will help you control your thought life is the rule of attention. Many people have found that it is very difficult, even nearly impossible, for them to completely exclude unwholesome thoughts from their minds. Such thoughts just seem to creep in of their own accord, and the more a person struggles to turn them out, the more entrenched they seem to become. How can we get every trace of evil out of our minds?

The secret of overcoming bad thoughts is to attend to what is good and thus crowd out negative thoughts. The surest cure for an unhealthy thought is a healthy one. This is why Paul declared to the Ephesian believers:

*Finally, brethren, whatsoever things are true, whatsoever things are honest, whatsoever things are just, whatsoever things are pure, whatsoever things are lovely, whatsoever things are of good report; if there be any virtue, and if there be any praise, think on these things. Those things, which ye have both learned, and received, and heard, and seen in me, do: and the God of peace shall be with you.*

Philippians 4:8-9

33

When you fill your minds with good thoughts, evil thoughts are driven away. When you keep your thinking high, the low "stuff" will find no place in you. So if you want to walk in victory, pay attention to the good "stuff."

Every time the devil tries to get in my way, I know what I need to do. I just tell him, "I don't have time for you. I'm so focused on these good things that there's no time for anything else." In this way, I obey the biblical command to *"resist the devil"*:

> *Submit yourselves therefore to God. Resist the devil, and he will flee from you.*
>
> James 4:7

I can tell you from experience that the devil hates the rule of attention. It drives him absolutely crazy.

## The Rule of Repetition

The third rule that will help you control your thought life is known as the rule of repetition. Most of us hate repetition, but nothing can help you more than repeating good thoughts over and over again. In this way, you can literally fill you mind with the promises of God found in His Word and, in the process, crowd out all harmful thoughts.

The devil knows how to use repetition too, but he uses it in a negative way. For example, when someone gets really mad at you, they seem compelled to say, "I hate you! I hate you! I hate you!" That's known as negative reinforcement.

When this happens to you, I dare you to recognize that the devil is trying to "mess" with your mind and to look that person in the face, smile, and say, "I love you! I love you! I love you!" That will get them every time.

### Are You Ready?

If you want God to do something in your life, then you have to be ready for Him to change your way of thinking. Forget about praying for your enemies to die. Forget about believing for every obstacle to move out of your way. Concentrate instead on getting your thinking right. Pull down those strongholds! Cast down those imaginations! Bring into captivity every thought to the obedience of Christ!

*If you want God to do something in your life, then you have to be ready for Him to change your way of thinking.*

Lock up those thoughts that are trying to destroy you and command them to stay in jail and not bother you any more. Put every bad thought into prison. While you're at it, give them a life sentence so they won't be able to trouble you anymore.

Or better yet, kill them all now. As it relates to your bad thoughts, capital punishment is good. If you simply put bad thoughts in jail, they may slip away again and try to do you harm. Every bad thought that has kept you bound must die.

Command bad thoughts to leave your home and your finances alone, and make your command in the powerful name of our Lord Jesus. Then start praising the Lord, and in this way show Him that you know that something good is about to happen in your life.

When the Lord steps in, He will bring you joy in the midst of your sorrow, and He will give you hope for your tomorrows. But he can't do that when He is opposed by your own thoughts. Cast them down now! Get them out of the way so that you can make progress.

You've been imagining way too much, and the devil has been magnifying your problems, until they now seem far too great to ever resolve. Those are all lies. Cast them down!

Like David, ask God to create a clean heart and a right spirit within you:

*Create in me a clean heart, O God; and renew a right spirit within me.*

Psalm 51:10

Believe for it, and begin to praise God for it. When the enemy is on your track, praise your way out of it.

Now that you know where the enemy attacks you, you can find victory over him, and your future can be bright. You must never again make the mistake of concentrating on external enemies. By recognizing the source of your conflict, you can learn to put to flight *The Enemy Inside Your Mind.*

Now that we know that truth is our most powerful weapon, let us examine in the coming chapters the truth as it relates to specific areas of our lives.

# CHAPTER 3

# Examining Yourself

———⊰⊱———

*And ye shall know the truth, and the truth shall make you free.*

John 8:32

The process necessary for victory over the enemy inside our minds is to reject his lies and accept the truth of God's Word and examine ourselves. Self-examination is important to every believer. We sometimes become so busy examining other people that we never take a good look at ourselves to determine if what we believe about ourselves is true or not.

Why is examining the truth about ourselves important? If the truth makes us free, then we need to know the truth—all of it. We need to know it, even if it hurts (and if often does).

When confronted with the need to reveal ourselves, we often resort to erecting walls. Self-examination never comes easily, but it's necessary if we are determined to live a victorious life.

*What you believe about yourself affects your emotions and eventually dictates your behavior.*

What you believe about yourself affects your emotions and eventually dictates your behavior. Many people have developed emotional problems simply because they're unable or unwilling to come to terms with themselves. When we fail to deal with ourselves honestly, we start to believe things about ourselves that are not true. In this way, we develop a false concept of ourselves, and this invites the presence of the enemy into our lives to control us.

### Examining the Falsehoods About Ourselves

Many people struggle to live normal lives, while burdened under the heavy weight of the lies they have come to believe about themselves. A lie can be fixed up so well that you believe it to be true. Reality, on the other hand, is the way things really are, as opposed to what we may believe to be true. Believing lies about ourselves can hide the truth of who we really are and keep the real person God has called us to be imprisoned within the confines of a false self-image.

Most of us have formed a picture in our minds of our idealized self, the person we dream about. But we cannot afford to live out our lives only seeing ourselves through the eyes of a perfect self. Instead, we must discover who we really are so that we can live a life of freedom and victory.

Believing a lie about ourselves can generate self-defeating behavior, and many live defeated lives because of it. Theirs is a most miserable existence, and it prevents them from achieving the things in life they desire to achieve and from becoming the person they want to become.

Our tendency to form in our minds the picture of our perfect self is a result of our unconscious need to be the way we were in the beginning, closely aligned with the image of our Creator. This causes many to think that they are either more or less than they really are. They develop a very mistaken concept of themselves.

We know who we want to be, and we know what we believe we can be (given the chance), but because we can't or don't accomplish the goals we set for ourselves, we come to feel that someone is holding us back. Someone is hindering us. What we fail to realize is that our own false concept of ourselves, the picture of our perfect self that we carry about in our minds, is what really hinders our progress.

So how do we sort it all out? How do we determine what truth really is? How do we separate who we really are from the false concepts about ourselves and the image of our perfect self we have come to accept? There has to be a starting point, and the proper starting point for believers is to examine our beliefs, our feelings, and our behavior based on the teachings of the eternal and unfailing Word of God.

What do you believe? Is it based on fact or fiction?

How do you feel on a daily basis? Are you basically happy? Or are you always sad? Clearly, the devil wants us depressed and to feel down. How did you feel when you got up this morning? How have you felt over the past few months? Is your mood consistent with the Christian life?

How about your behavior? Be honest. If it hasn't been what it should be, then it needs attention. To lie to yourself about this will only hinder your progress. If you've been fired from ten jobs in the last ten months, and you're still blaming your inability to keep a job on the fact that your supervisors just don't like you, maybe you need to turn the spotlight onto your own behavior. It may not have been the ten employers who were at fault; it may have been you. Admit this, and you will have taken a giant step toward a resolution of your long-standing problem.

We have examined others long enough. It's now time that we took a good look at ourselves.

Once we recognize what we really believe about ourselves, we must then ask ourselves if what we believe about ourselves is true or false. You may think you're great and even more than great, but is it true? Truth produces positiveness, confidence, and satisfaction, but lies produce just the opposite. Entertaining lies keeps you feeling nervous and unfulfilled.

Again, it is important to examine ourselves. What will truth do? It will create self-acceptance, just as a lie will produce self-rejection.

Have you accepted yourself or have you rejected yourself? Do you like who you are? Or do you secretly want to be somebody else? Maybe the reason you get so angry with other people is that you're secretly not happy with who *you* are. This is true in many cases. When we walk in truth, we learn to accept who we are, and there is no more self-rejection.

### Traits of Self-Acceptance and Self-Rejection

It might be helpful to examine some of the common traits of a self-accepting person. Self-accepting people tend to be real, honest, open, secure, loving, confident, and responsible. The reason they can be so secure in what they do and in who they are is that they have accepted themselves.

This does not necessarily mean that other people have accepted them, but they have accepted themselves—whatever other people think. Before any of us can move forward in our lives, we must begin to like who we are. We must accept ourselves.

When we accept ourselves, we become secure. We don't care if someone laughs at the color of our suit. In our minds, it's the person who is laughing who has the problem, not us. The self-accepting person knows that they look good.

Self-accepting people are not moved by what other people think because they've learned to accept themselves and who they are. They're no longer wrestling with their true identity. They like who they are and are glad God made them that way. All of us need to reach this point in our lives, because this is where we begin to walk in true freedom.

Too many of us, because we have not accepted ourselves, have erected emotional walls around ourselves. This may explain why we have trouble loving a neighbor, or why, in church, we rush out before the benediction is pronounced so that we won't have to greet everyone. When we accept ourselves, then we're able to accept the people around us as well.

I encounter a surprising number of people, even Christians, who have low self-esteem and don't like who they are. This is so crazy. As Christians, we have every reason to like who we are. After all, God made us, and He doesn't make any junk. How about you? Are you walking in self-acceptance or self-rejection?

Those who walk in self-rejection tend to show signs of self-doubt. They always wear masks. You may see them smiling, but they aren't really smiles. They are masks they're wearing.

Self-rejecting people are full of anxiety and are often depressed. They're up one day and down the next—all because they don't like who they are.

Such people are also usually full of guilt and distrust towards others. They find it hard to trust others because they can't trust themselves and also because they've been hurt in the past and don't want to be hurt again. They reject others because they reject themselves.

When we make mistakes in life, this often opens a door for the devil to cause us to dislike ourselves, but self-accepting people never reject themselves because of past mistakes. They simply make up their minds that the next time they will deal with the situation better. Having made a mistake may make them more careful the next time, but it won't stop them from continuing to appreciate who God has made them to be. And they will never allow their own failures to keep them from trusting others.

This is important because we have thought that our problem was gaining the acceptance of others. The real problem is learning to accept ourselves.

Those who are self-rejecting tend to be drawn into co-dependencies and addictions. They must have something or someone to reassure them of who they are. Some drink in excess and get drunk because they need reassurance. They believe if they drink that bottle of liquor they'll be able to forget about their problems. The problem is that when they have gotten drunk they like themselves even less. The devil constantly plays these kinds of games with our minds, so be honest. Know who you are and learn to like who you are.

The devil loves for us to erect emotional walls around ourselves to keep us isolated from others. When we meet those who seem to be argumentative, angry, and down-right mean, it may be that they're not really mean people at all. Very possibly they just dislike who they are, and the only way they know to protect themselves emotionally is by acting in this strange way. Hopefully this doesn't describe you, but if it does, you have some work to do on yourself.

To be totally honest, all of us have some work to do in this area. If we think we don't, God can give us a more true insight into our real character. We all have some changes that need to be made. But as long as we continue to reject some things about ourselves, our lives can never improve.

### *Learning to Accept Who You Are*

If we could just learn to accept ourselves, God could use us more. This may be the reason some people go to church only when they feel like it. They haven't yet accepted themselves as really being important. And most of us don't yet know how important it is that we fill the seats we're intended to fill every time we go to church.

God has us in His house of worship for a purpose. He may have us there to minister to someone beside us, but some are not present when God needs them in this way because they have it in their minds that it won't matter if they go or not. This is erroneous thinking.

What if I, as a pastor, thought that way? What if I failed to attend church for a month because I thought it wouldn't matter if I was there or not? I'm needed at church, not just because I'm the pastor, but because I'm a part of a ministry. And because I'm part of a ministry, I have an important part to play in that ministry. Each part is important because it takes a whole body to make any program work.

There are no big I's and little you's in the body of Christ. Each of us is important, and each of us must accept the fact that we are important. I'm important, for I'm part of the number that makes the body of Christ work, but you're just as important. Accept and appreciate who you are in the church, and then take responsibility accordingly.

We always want someone else to take the responsibility, and we even want to blame our lack of success on someone else's failure to support us in some way. But God has given each of us the personal responsibility to make whatever changes need to be made in our lives so that we can live in victory. Become responsible for your own inner peace and contentment, and stop looking to others.

*Concentrate on making positive changes in your life and going to the next level, and don't worry about whether or not others can see it.*

Concentrate on making positive changes in your life and going to the next level, and don't worry about whether or not others can see it. Continue working on the process of becoming who God has created and called you to be, and others will notice in due time. In the meantime, accept yourself even if others don't.

Do you realize how long it takes for someone who knows what you used to be to accept the fact that you've changed? When they see you living right and doing well they still insist on saying, "Child, I knew them when they were out there living any kind of way. Who are they trying to fool?" But if you know that you've changed, why get upset about what others say? Why worry about what anyone else thinks about you? It doesn't matter if they accept you or not— just as long as you're in Christ, and you've learned to accept yourself.

Personally, I long ago stopped caring if people accepted me or not. It doesn't matter to me. And this is the attitude we all must have.

Stop crying every night because someone has told you that you're ugly. Refuse to allow any human being to put you into a state of depression over your looks. Just look at yourself in the mirror and say, "I know who I am. God made me who I am, and I'm beautiful. Beauty is more than skin deep." You can do it.

### Become Aware of What You're Missing

A giant step that you can make toward positive change is to be aware that you're missing out on a dimension of life that others are already enjoying. This is not to say that you should be jealous of what somebody else has, but that you should desire those good things in your life. You can do this without entertaining envy in your heart.

Not long after I bought my first Cadillac (a white-on-white model), a brother pulled up beside me one day and rolled his window down. I was sure he was going to say something nice about my car, but he must have known that I was a preacher, because he said to me, "Jesus didn't ride in no Cadillac."

"No," I answered, "Jesus didn't ride in a Cadillac, but He did ride on a cloud, and this was the closest thing I could find to it."

About two years after that, I stopped at a traffic light one day, and there beside me in a Cadillac, with a big smile on his face, was the same man who had made that critical comment. Then it dawned on me what his problem had been. He hadn't been against preachers driving Cadillacs. His problem had been that he didn't have one himself.

We must understand that we can't get what God has for us when we're jealous of what someone else has. The best thing to do is to appreciate what someone else has and realize that what God has for you is on the way. Rather than be jealous of others, go to them and say, "I see that the Lord is blessing you. Tell me how to get these same blessings?" Find out their secret rather than simply thinking badly of them because they're blessed.

Take a positive step by having an awareness that you're missing out on a dimension of life that others have. You can have the self-acceptance and freedom you see others enjoying, but you must be willing to make the required changes in your life in order to receive them.

### Be Willing to Make the Required Changes

Many people want what someone else has, but they don't want to make the changes necessary to receive it. For instance, some preachers want a church just like the one I pastor in New Orleans. The problem is that they don't want to live a disciplined life. They don't want to study to show themselves approved the way they need to in order to accomplish it (see 2 Timothy 2:15).

If you desire to have certain things in life, it doesn't do you any good to get mad at the people who already have them. You can have them too, but first you have to make some changes.

Some people are simply not willing to change. The years come and go, and they remain the same. Change is not comfortable for them.

Change is not easy for any of us, but when you become determined to do better, that's already a positive change. It is then that God can step in to help you correct the things that are wrong in your life.

I figured out a long time ago that if things are going wrong in my life, it's not God's fault. Therefore, when something isn't right, I never waste time blaming Him. Instead, I take a good look at myself to try and discover what the problem is. It's sure to be in me.

*The Bible has declared that truth sets us free, so accept the truth and allow it to make the necessary adjustments in your life.*

You can't just sit back and say, "I didn't do well last year or the year before, and so I'm not even going to attempt to do better this year." If you think that way, the devil will keep you in a rut from now on. You'll never go to the next level that God is trying to take you to. The Bible has declared that truth sets us free, so accept the truth and allow it to make the necessary adjustments in your life.

Change does not come easily, and it certainly doesn't happen spontaneously, so we must have patience and take it step by step as it comes. For instance, every time I get overweight I wish I could somehow lose those extra pounds in just a few days or weeks, but I know that it doesn't happen that way. If I want to lose the extra pounds, I have to go through the process. It doesn't do me any good to get upset about that fact. It's my own fault, and I've brought the problem on myself. So if someone says, "Wow! You've put on some weight!" what can I say? It's true, and I just need to get it off.

"Don't worry," I tell them. "I'm working on it." But I know that it will take time. In the exact same way, spiritual change does not come overnight, but if we're doing the things that are necessary for our lives to get back on the right track and we're walking in truth, those changes will eventually come.

Change is a decision and it reflects intention. We must become intentional about changing our self-defeating behavior. We must be determined to do better than we've been doing, to think better than we've been thinking about ourselves, and to experience the things God wants to do in our lives. He knows that we're His special children, and it's time that we knew it too. He said:

> *But ye are a chosen generation, a royal priesthood, an holy nation, a peculiar people; that ye should show forth the praises of him who hath called you out of darkness into his marvellous light.*
>
> 1 Peter 2:9

As God's special child, you are the only person in the world who can accept the responsibility for making changes in your life. No one else can do that for you. If you will decide to walk in these truths, you can begin to move from self-rejection to self-acceptance, and your life will change. Stop blaming the circumstances you happen to find yourself in on the people around you and realize that only you can change you.

You might want to have some counseling sessions with your pastor or another trusted spiritual advisor, and this may help. But, in the end, you are the only one who can make it all happen.

## Raise Your Standards

Once you accept responsibility for your own decisions and understand who you are in Christ, you must then raise your standards. Make up your mind that you will no longer do the things you used to do that caused you to live in self-rejection...that you will no longer go the places you used to go, but should not have gone. In this way, you're raising the bar.

There were arguments that you had before that you'll no longer have. You've raised the standard. If you fail to do this, you'll always remain at the same level. And that's just what the devil wants.

Remaining stagnant, at the same level, for too long will one day put you into a state of depression. When you look back years from now and realize that you're still in the same place you were years before, you will hate yourself for it. Get started toward that next level now.

## Confront Your Lies

Don't be willing to settle for anything short of reality. Life is too short to constantly be living in a fantasy world. It's time to confront your myths.

The first reality you must face is the fact that your perfect self only exists in your dreams. Therefore, exchange your perfect self for the real thing and accept yourself as you really are. Trying to make your perfect self reality will keep you in defeat. Deal with reality.

For example, accept the fact that you don't have a perfect family. I would love to have a family like that of Ozzie and Harriet, but I don't, so why should I lament that fact? Theirs may have been the ideal, but mine is the real.

Having every member of the house together at the breakfast table is nice, but not all of us can have that. Having no arguments when everyone comes home in the evening is nice, but not all of us have that. A household in which everyone is happy all the time would be nice, but that's not the reality of the twenty-first century. So why should I struggle against it? Trying to live in a perfect world instead of the real world won't work.

That's not to say that we should not strive for the perfect. My real world will always press toward my perfect world, but I can't get to my perfect world before I deal with the real one. I can't expect my real world to always come up to the standards of my perfect world, but day by day, as I deal with reality, my real world becomes better and better.

Get this balance. If you stop pressing toward the goal of your perfect world, your real world can become disheartening. But exchange your perfect self for your real self so that you can gain self-acceptance for the journey. Know where you're going in life, but also know where you actually are at the present. Then you can work to perfect yourself.

That's not to say that I should boast of where I am now. It's just to say that I need to know where I am so I can know where I'm going.

The constant gap between the perfect self and the real self can be a cause for anxiety and discouragement. This is why it's so important that we learn to effectively deal with the real world.

I often encounter pastors whose ideal is to one day have a church like the one I pastor with thousands of members. Their problem is that they want it now. When they come to me depressed because their church hasn't reached that level yet, I tell them that their focus should be on realistically dealing with where they are now, not on what they may be in the future. There's no reason for them to become depressed because their ministry hasn't yet reached the level of Greater St. Stephen. They don't understand what I had to go through to get where I am with this ministry, and they must deal with the reality of their own world.

If a pastor has fifty people, they can't expect to do what I can do with many thousands of members. When pastors begin to understand that, they can be happy with the members they currently have and what that enables them to do, rather than being depressed because they only have that many. Instead of looking at me and what God has done with Greater St. Stephen, they should begin to thank God for the fifty members they have, and when they begin to thank Him for the fifty, He'll begin to multiply their numbers. Deal with truth, and don't beat yourself up because you don't have the ideal yet.

### Walk in Freedom As the Real You

The real you may be imprisoned within the walls of a false self. This can be a serious problem if, for instance, you believe the lie that you have to prove to others that you are somebody. This might cause you to run around like a crazy person for the rest of your life, trying to please everyone around you, and not accomplishing much. You're God's special child, with a unique purpose and destiny, and, therefore, you need not prove anything to anyone.

It doesn't matter what other people think or say. For instance, it doesn't matter to me if the Ku Klux Klan doesn't like me or what they might say about me. Does anyone think for a moment that just because some member of the KKK might say I'm nothing that I am nothing? Of course not. We must learn to appreciate ourselves regardless of what other people think about us.

Pause for a moment and ask the Holy Spirit to guide you as you begin to search for your true self. Ask Him to help you recognize and accept truth when and where you find it—even if it hurts. Jesus said:

> *Howbeit when he, the Spirit of truth, is come, he will guide you into all truth.*
>
> John 16:13

When the Holy Spirit comes into your heart, if you need direction and guidance, He will furnish it. He will guide you into *"all truth,"* and that includes all truth about yourself.

The real you does not have to prove that you are somebody. You don't have to buy people things to prove who you are. You don't have to do something for them in order to try to win them over. Be who you are, trusting God to make you the very best person you can be.

Accept yourself as you are today, and work to make yourself what you want to be tomorrow. This change in attitude will produce a corresponding change in everything about your life.

Be glad that God made you who you are, and know that whatever people say, no one can beat you at being you. You're the very best you that exists in the world today. You're a special child in God's sight. Believe it, speak it into your life, and begin to walk in it. Tell God, "I thank You, Lord, that You made me who I am," and mean it.

In this way, by knowing the truth about yourself, you will put to flight *The Enemy Inside Your Mind*.

CHAPTER 4

# Moving toward Maturity in Examining Yourself

*I know whom I have believed, and am persuaded that he is able to keep that which I have committed unto him against that day.*

2 Timothy 1:12

Examining ourselves is so important that it's surprising how many people are never real with themselves. We will continue to face problems in our lives just as long as we fail to learn how to be truthful—with ourselves and with others.

Truth brings freedom, Jesus said. Knowing truth means coming to know ourselves, and our knowing comes from understanding, experiencing, and having a personal knowledge of the reality of our everyday existence.

It's impossible to really know something that's not true. There may be certain things we think or believe, but we can only know those things that are definitely true. If we're to move out of the prison of our myths and into the freedom of reality, we must shift from merely believing into knowing truth.

## The Shift from Believing to Knowing

According to the Bible, we come to Christ and become one of His followers by believing:

*And [he, the Philippian jailer] said, Sirs, what must I do to be saved? And they [Paul and Silas] said, believe on the Lord Jesus Christ, and thou shalt be saved, and thy house.*

Acts 16:30-31

We come to Christ by believing, but then, after that start, we must shift from believing to knowing. This is why Paul could say that he knew whom he had believed and was persuaded of His ability to keep him. He had first accepted these things by faith, but now he knew them to be true. If we only believe and never come to know, we can still go down the wrong path in life.

This is what happens to me sometimes when I'm driving with my wife. She's a wonderfully convincing backseat driver, and sometimes she says to me something like, "Honey, turn left here." Even though I believe that

I'm going the right way, I follow her directions, but the result is that we sometimes end up in the wrong place.

I'm not blaming her. If I knew where I was going in the first place and told her so, it would help us to avoid all the confusion.

When you really know something, nobody can confuse you about it. This, again, is why we must shift from believing to knowing. Believing is good, but when you know something to be true, it makes all the difference in your life.

As we have seen, it's also possible to believe something to be true when it's not true. Just because we believe something is true doesn't make it so. Therefore, we must carefully examine our beliefs in order to discover and know the truth about ourselves. What we believe is not always true, but what we know always is. This brings us to the subject of the old self and the new self.

### The Old Self and the New Self

There is an old self, and there is a new self. The old self functions on the falsehoods we believe about ourselves, and the new self functions on reality. It is the false beliefs produced by our old self that cause us to harbor feelings of self-rejection and shame. These feelings are generated from the myths we have been taught or have otherwise come to believe about ourselves over time.

As long as we rely on our old self to define who we are and what we believe, we can deem things to be true that are not true. You may believe, for example, that because of the color of your skin you could never accomplish certain things in life. Because of who you are or where you came from, you already have set in your mind the things that you feel you can or cannot accomplish. This attack on your mind is nothing but a trick of the enemy to hinder you. Many people reject themselves and are ashamed of who they are because their old self produces this kind of self-rejection.

Although our old self relies on our myths to tell us who we are and how we're supposed to behave, the new self relies on reality. And this is where I am trying to take you with this book—to the level of relying on what's real, not imagined. It doesn't concern me that your reality may be stark and that it may hurt you to deal with it. You simply must get off of Fantasy Island and learn the truth.

As we begin to rely on what we know to be true about ourselves, reality will begin to positively influence our behavior, producing self-appreciation and acceptance. As we have established, if our lives are to change for the better, we must first learn to like ourselves. And the only way we can learn to like ourselves is to be true to ourselves.

This is what reality is all about. We must look at life the way it is, and then deal with it on that basis.

### Developing the New You

As we deal with reality and truth, we will begin to experience improvement in our lives. If we refuse to be honest with ourselves and we cling to the lies that we have, until now, accepted as truth, we will never see improvement. This would delight the devil. He wants to keep us down by influencing us to rely on our old selves, never coming to the realization of who we really are.

On the other hand, there is God, who wants to let us know how very special and significant we really are. If we're to walk in the freedom of reality, we must change our thinking and thus our feelings and behavior, as we shift from operating in the old self to operating in the new self.

This process begins, as we have already established, with examining what we believe, how we feel, and how we behave. This does not refer to the façade we sometimes put on when somebody asks us how we're feeling. We say we're just fine—even when we know deep down that something is bothering us. Our protests of being fine are not reality, and reality is what we must deal with.

The positive feelings generated from the new self are the result of coming to know the truth about ourselves and then making positive behavioral changes. For example, if you're a mean person, once you acknowledge the fact that you have a mean disposition, change can occur. As long as you go around acting mean but refusing to acknowledge the fact that you *are* mean, change cannot come. If we're not willing to admit what our problems are, how can we confront them?

The person with a mean disposition may notice, in looking at their family tree, that their mother or their grandfather was mean, and that the spirit of meanness has been passed on to them. Nevertheless, once truth is dealt with, positive changes can be made—regardless of what may have been passed down to us from previous generations.

Whatever the case may be, we must be willing to deal with the truth of our need. If the majority of the people you come in contact with tell you that you're mean, maybe you need to examine whether or not it may be true and deal with it if it is. Victory comes through dealing with truth.

The people who don't want to hear the truth must not want to move to the next level in their lives, because that's what's required. We cannot afford to ignore the truth when it is presented to us.

*The people who don't want to hear the truth must not want to move to the next level in their lives, because that's what's required.*

How do we start the process of changing from our old self to our new self? The first step is having a desire to change. Without this desire, a person can remain the same for thirty, forty, or even sixty years. And then what happens? They die and pass that generational curse down to someone else in their immediate family—all because they have refused to change.

Developing a desire to change may be difficult, but it's necessary if we want freedom for ourselves and for future generations. As we've already discussed, we must become thoroughly worn out and disgusted with the way we are. We must become tired of the mask-wearing, self-rejection, and shame. And until we get to that point, little or no change will occur.

If we continue to go back and forth, thinking that maybe we're not as bad as we thought we were, we will stay in the same old rut. If we're hateful and mean, and we know it, we must deal with being hateful and mean.

We must become so disgusted with the way we are that we're finally able to shed all the trappings of the old misinformed self.

### Reversing the Negative Effects of Misinformation

It's surprising what some people have taken into their minds and accepted as truth, causing them to be totally misinformed about themselves. Someone may have said some negative things about you in the past, and, because of that, you may now be misinformed and not like who you are. And if you don't like who you are, you won't expect others to like you either. This may make it difficult for you to make friends or to develop other types of healthy relationships.

As you grew up, someone in your family may have told you that you were "nothing." Your parents may have been overheard to say that they wished they had never had you. Or a teacher may have made some unkind remark about you. If so, you may be dealing with a misinformed you, a you that really believes you're no good. It's time to cast aside such misinformation and to embrace God's truth about you.

Being misinformed is not a sin. You did nothing wrong. Still, misinformation can become a curse that keeps you bound with constant and nearly unbearable feelings of inadequacy. Misinformed people are usually awkward and self-conscious around others.

Among every race of people, there are many who are misinformed. This is true of the Caucasians who believe that all black people are bad. This belief, of course, is a myth. There are many very good black people. But even though not all black people are bad, I've noticed, as a black man, that when I'm around some Caucasian people, they become very nervous.

One day, for instance, I stepped into an elevator in which an elderly white lady was riding. I could see the fear that came over her face when I got in. She immediately grabbed her purse and moved to the back of the elevator and stood tight against the wall. Her reaction was so obvious that I turned and said to her, "Whatever it is that you have there, I don't want it. And there's a good possibility that I have more than you do." The fear and mistrust she felt that day was all in her mind.

But most of us would react to others in the very same way if we were misinformed. We, for instance, sometimes walk into a room full of people, and we suddenly think that everyone in the room is looking at us or talking about us. Some, who are very paranoid in this way, may even turn to a person who has not been paying any attention to them at all and ask, "What are you looking at?" Misinformation leads to this type of anxiety.

I trust that you're tired of living with constant anxiety and ready to learn to like who you are. If so, stop trying to change who you are when you're around other people.

Some even go to the extreme of changing the way they talk and act when they're around people of other races, simply because they don't feel comfortable with who they are. It's time to rid ourselves of all self-doubt, guilt, and shame that has built up over the years because we've been deceived, manipulated, put down, used, or abused.

Many of you who are reading this book can undoubtedly say that at some point in your life you have been manipulated. You didn't want it to happen, but it happened anyway. You may have been deceived. You may have been put down or abused. But whatever you may have faced in the past, it's time to know the truth about yourself and come to grips with who you really are. This can be a life-changing experience.

Why is it that some people absolutely refuse to deal with reality? They block out truth, and because of it, they never grow or experience improvement in their lives. Some, because they have been put down or criticized in the past regarding their ability to learn, never attempt to learn anything new. For example, many are afraid to even attempt to use a computer because of being put down or laughed at when they attempted to learn something new in the past. How sad!

People like these seem to become comfortable at their level of accomplishment in life and never press forward into anything new. They'll never go to the next level because they're afraid to try. They're afraid that if they do try new things, someone may make fun of them again. This is very limiting behavior. It's time to come to know ourselves, to confront our myths, and to deal with reality.

## Learning to Appreciate the New You

I want every man and woman, boy and girl, who reads this book to be able to take pride in who they are and to stop looking at other people around them and wishing they were them instead. Until we can begin to appreciate who we are, the grass will always look greener on the other side of the fence. Learn to appreciate where God has placed you.

When we fail to appreciate who we are and where God has placed us, we start putting ourselves down, putting our city down, and putting everything else around us down. And as we continue to think and speak negatively about ourselves and our environment, these thoughts become imbedded into our minds, and they will keep us down—unless and until we decide to make a change.

Instead of thinking negatively about your lot in life, stop and say, "Wait a minute! I'm a human being, and I have to get up and make something of myself. It doesn't matter what city I'm in. I will be the best I can be in this city."

When this kind of positive thinking catches on, it makes a difference in any community. But if no one in the community decides to deal with reality and recognize that one individual can make a difference, everyone in the community will continue to run from who they are and what they can do.

Over the years, it was drilled into the people of our African-American churches that there were certain things they could never hope to achieve. Consequently, every time I tried to do certain things as pastor of a predominately African-American church, I ran up against these myths. This went on until I got tired of it and decided that I no longer wanted to be average. I no longer wanted to live under the myth of what our church could and could not achieve. What did people know anyway? If God said we could achieve it, then we *could* achieve it.

And, because we refused to accept the common myths about ourselves and our potential, we *did* achieve it.

This is the kind of mentality that will set each of us free. You must get up one day with the determination to stop settling for second best. God has created you to be the best that you can be, and if you will decide to accept His will and work toward fulfilling it, you can bring it to pass.

Success *can* happen in your life. You don't have to spend the rest of your life looking longingly to the other side of the fence and seeing what someone else has or what they have done. Thank God for what you have and then begin to appreciate it and use it for His glory. And when you thus learn to deal with the reality of yourself, things will begin to turn around for you.

### The Advantage of the Believer— The Resource of a Renewed Mind

Christians have many advantages over the world (the nonbelievers) in learning to accept truth, overcome myths, and walk in reality. One of the greatest of these advantages is that we have the resource of a renewed mind to support us in our search for self-truth. If you don't know Jesus Christ, this process is difficult. But when you know Him, you have the support system of a renewed mind that can help you in your search.

Having a renewed mind, in fact, is the only way to get to know the real you. Paul wrote to the believers in Rome:

*I beseech you therefore, brethren, by the mercies of God, that ye present your bodies a living sacrifice, holy, acceptable unto God, which is your reason-able service. And be not conformed to this world: but be ye transformed by the renewing of your mind, that ye may prove what is that good, and acceptable, and perfect, will of God.*

Romans 12:1-2

As I noted previously, it doesn't matter what state your mind may be in; it can be renewed. And through the renewing of your mind, you can come out of your world of myths into the reality of knowing the truth about yourself and your potential in life.

This biblical passage assures us that we don't have to remain prisoners of misinformed minds. Instead, we can take control of our wrong thinking. Once we discover that we have the resource of God's Word available to us to renew our minds, we must use it to confront and replace our myths with truth.

## Knowing vs. Experiencing

Knowing what should be done and doing it, of course, are two very different things. Once we know the truth, we must be willing to act upon what we have learned. There must be a behavioral change. This is not to say that everything must change at once, but there must be some evidence that we are changing as we are exposed to the truth of God's Word.

Again, change will not happen overnight, but at least we've started the process of change, and if we continue the process, the desired result will eventually come. So be patient. For example, if you have a bad temper, I'm not suggesting that you'll never again "go off," but at least your "going off" should happen less and less as you act upon what you've learned. Be willing to wait for your feelings about yourself to catch up with the process, but in the meantime, be determined to never again allow a bad temper to control you.

The reason some who know the truth of God's Word remain the same is that they tire of the process of striving to do better. But if our desire to change is strong enough, we will not tire of the process that brings it about. Instead, we will refuse to continue living in bondage to the old self. Why settle for living with myths when we have the ability to make life better?

As children of God, we have to believe that further change is possible because of the great change that has already taken place in our lives. If anybody should know about change, it's those who are believers. This is not to say that we're perfect, but at least we're better than we were when we were living in sin. And if we're better now than we were when we were living in sin, then we must realize that if God could change us from what we were, then He can definitely cause us to continue the process of change.

Believing for this type of change is extremely difficult for a sinner who has never yet experienced the change that comes with salvation. But when you become a child of God, you should already know something about being changed. Paul wrote:

*Therefore if any man be in Christ, he is a new creature: old things are passed away; behold, all things are become new.*

2 Corinthians 5:17

Christians can change more because they have already been changed; that's reality. I've been changed, and therefore I can change more. We must speak that with our mouths and believe it in our hearts.

If you were negative before, move toward being positive, for you have been given the power to make the necessary change. If you don't think so, consider just how powerful God has made us. He created us just *"a little lower than the angels"*:

> *What is man, that thou art mindful of him? and the son of man, that thou visitest him? For thou hast made him a little lower than the angels, and hast crowned him with glory and honour. Thou madest him to have dominion over the works of thy hands; thou hast put all things under his feet: All sheep and oxen, yea, and the beasts of the field; The fowl of the air, and the fish of the sea, and whatsoever passeth through the paths of the seas. O Lord our Lord, how excellent is thy name in all the earth!*
>
> Psalm 8:4-9

Have you come to realize how very awesome it is to be a human being? What a privilege you have!

And, even better than that, have you considered how very awesome it is to be a redeemed human being? God has made you *"a little lower than the angels,"* not a little lower than a dog. So it's time to step up to the plate with boldness and determine that your pity-party days are over.

I don't believe in pity parties because I understand the many promises of God's Word to each of us as believers.

One of my favorite promises, one that seems to say it all, is found in John's letter to the churches. He said:

*Ye are of God, little children, and have overcome them: because greater is he that is in you, than he that is in the world.*

1 John 4:4

The Greater One lives inside of us, and we need to start acting like it. If He doesn't yet live inside of you, you need to acknowledge that and recognize that you need God's presence on the inside. That's dealing with reality. But if He's in you already, He should be able to do something in your life to change you and make you better.

*The Greater One lives inside of us, and we need to start acting like it.*

### Change Brings with It the Needed Resources

Inward change from the old person to the new person in Christ brings with it all the resources needed for changing our self-defeating thinking and behavior. If you are in Christ and defeat still keeps happening over and over again in your life, you must deal with the reality of you and stop blaming your defeat on somebody else. You must be true to yourself and examine why you keep encountering defeat—when, in reality, you have the resources at your disposal that are necessary to live in victory.

As we noted in Chapter 2, we have been supplied with all the resources we need to help us be victorious in any situation we may encounter in life. We believers have so much more than the world. For instance, we have the assurances of God's Word. Personally, this is what keeps me going. I don't know how I would make it without the treasures of God's Word to sustain me.

One Sunday night, while ministering in our church, I began to feel quite ill. I told the devil that he was a liar, because I was determined to finish my message. And I did finish because I had the assurance of God's Word, and it sustained me.

When you have the assurance of God's Word, you can face any situation that comes your way. You can even lose a loved one and know how to handle what to most of us is one of life's most difficult situations—all because of the assurances God has given you.

In order to make these promises effective in our lives, first we must learn them, and second, we must claim them as our own. This is why it's so important that we get all the Word we possibly can inside of us.

### The Importance of Living Daily with the Assurance of God's Word

When was the last time someone came up to you and said, "Wow! You're going to a whole new level in God! I can see it!"? When someone looks at you, do they see the same old person you've always been? When we truly have the assurance of God's Word, it will produce results, and someone will eventually notice a new attitude in us. His Word enables us to experience positive change in our lives.

If you're in Christ and in God's Word, at some point the new you should become visible. The Word of God is just that powerful. That's why I spend time reading it over and over. There I find many things that help me in my Christian journey. All of us need the truths of God's Word to help us be victorious in this life.

Jesus sent the Holy Spirit to teach us about the Father and the Son, but also to show us things that would properly direct our lives. He is *"the Spirit of truth"* (see John 16:13), and so when the Holy Spirit comes, we're able to accept and deal with truth. This is why it's so important to have a real relationship with God through His Holy Spirit.

When we have this type of relationship with God, we can begin to recognize the unlimited potential we have in Christ, and we can begin to gain other new insights into ourselves. This enables us to change our self-defeating behavior and to enjoy new feelings about ourselves and our future in God.

As we go through life's journey, our heavenly Father wants us to feel good about ourselves. That's why we must begin liking who we are and come to the point that we are able to thank God for making us who we are, instead of being constantly disappointed with our lot in life.

## More Good News

These are the simple truths God has inspired me to share with you in this book. I want you to understand that our union with Christ is not just to save us from our sins and provide us with a ticket to heaven. Although even that seems like more than we could ever hope for, there is more good news. God intended for us to begin enjoying the benefits of His work on the cross right now in this lifetime. You can, in fact, start enjoying these benefits today, this very hour.

We're God's children, and as His children, we're entitled to walk in all the benefits that He provides for us. As we obey His will, we should expect to receive what is rightfully ours.

It's time that we recognize the fact that God is ready to meet every need we have through our relationship with Him in Christ. Many believers still live under the myth that even though they serve the Lord, they can never get ahead in life. We must deal with reality and let our assurance be the Word of God. It declares:

*He that spared not his own Son, but delivered him up for us all, how shall he not with him also freely give us all things?*

Romans 8:32

Do you think that God would refuse to provide you with something you need when He's already given us Christ? His Word expresses the fact that He wants to give us everything we need in life, and, indeed, has already made provision for it:

*According as his divine power hath given unto us all things that pertain unto life and godliness, through the knowledge of him that hath called us to glory and virtue.*

2 Peter 1:3

We must stop believing lies about our future and know and understand this truth. It is God's promise to us, and it, therefore, cannot fail. He delights in supplying the things we need:

*But my God shall supply all your need according to his riches in glory by Christ Jesus.*

Philippians 4:19

We don't have to wait for the next life to begin our recovery from the fall in Eden. God intends for us to start experiencing the process of recovery right now in this life. Then we can expect its completion in the next life. Start enjoying the benefits of His Word through salvation now, and then expect to experience complete recovery when you get to glory. God's will for you is that you experience and enjoy a taste of heaven right now as you prepare for heaven later. You were meant to enjoy this life.

When these great promises are spoken to us, there is always another voice that accuses us of failure and of ineligibility for the very blessings of God we are claiming. That voice can only be quieted by the voice of God through His Word. God's promises leave the devil in silence. For instance, God's Word promises me:

*I can do all things through Christ which strengtheneth me.*

Philippians 4:13

Every time the voice of discouragement and condemnation comes to make us believe we can't achieve success in life because of our past, we must speak the truth of God's Word. And we must believe and know that success is ours because of who we are in Christ. As long as we are in Him, we're free from condemnation, and success is guaranteed. Paul declared:

*Who is he that condemneth? It is Christ that died, yea rather, that is risen again, who is even at the right hand of God, who also maketh intercession for us.*

Romans 8:34

Christ will not condemn us; He wants to bless us. He is interceding, or pleading, on our behalf. He's taking our case and our needs before the Father.

If you need a lawyer, Jesus is the best one you could possibly have. When He pleads your case, you will win. And the Scriptures show us that this is exactly what He is doing right now before the Father:

*We have an advocate with the Father, Jesus Christ the righteous.*

1 John 2:1

So Jesus is not condemning us. To the contrary, He has become our advocate.

It's time that we come to know who we are. We're not nobodies who always seem to get all the bad breaks in life.

No matter what we face, we must understand that every test we go through is for a reason. I don't have time to grumble and complain about everything I've had to deal with in life. I know that I went through it all for a reason, and every situation that I've faced in my life has made me better.

74

Some of you may be going through something right now. But you can turn that seemingly negative situation around by recognizing that you're going through that situation for a reason, and when you come out of it, you'll come out like Job, *"as gold"*:

> *But he knoweth the way that I take: when he hath tried me, I shall come forth as gold.*
>
> Job 23:10

You will come forth from the trials of life with a testimony, with victory, and with a shout of praise to God. Oh, we're not nobodies; we're victorious in Christ Jesus. In this way, by moving toward maturity in the truth about yourself, you will put to flight *The Enemy Inside Your Mind.*

# CHAPTER 5

# The Truth About People Pleasers

=➤-◊-◄=

*Therefore, I urge you, brothers, in view of God's mercy, to offer your bodies as living sacrifices, holy and pleasing to God—this is your spiritual act of worship. Do not conform any longer to the pattern of this world, but be transformed by the renewing of your mind. Then you will be able to test and approve what God's will is—his good, pleasing and perfect will.*

Romans 12:1-2, NIV

### Characteristics of a People Pleaser

Keeping us in bondage through the fear of rejection is one of the favorite tricks of the enemy. All of us are valuable, regardless of who does or does not like us, and we must come to know and understand just how valuable we are. We're valuable because God made us valuable—not because someone likes us.

As I established early on, far too many people live their lives with feelings of low self-worth because they're convinced that they're unimportant. This is a lie that has been drilled into them, probably early in life, and probably by someone who has rejected them. Often the result is that they become people pleasers and live their lives just to keep everyone else happy. At the same time, they neglect their own happiness. What a miserable existence this must be!

This is not God's plan for any of our lives, especially for those of us who call ourselves Christians. If anybody should be happy, it should be God's children. It's wrong to carry the burden of trying to make everyone else happy while, at the same time, denying your own happiness.

Some of you might confess, "My entire family depends upon me. I have to keep everybody else happy, so I don't have any time for myself." If this is your confession, you have a problem, and you need to deal with it. You must face the truth that it's not your assignment in life to keep everybody else in the world happy.

A people pleaser's association with others is usually not a happy one. This is because they never truly express their feelings and ideas for fear of being rejected or not being liked. We have found that such people don't make good committee members. Too often they leave committee meetings without ever having expressed their own thoughts and ideas.

People pleasers are often abused by others. For instance, I think it's a shame for a husband, after his wife has been nice enough to pre-pare his breakfast, to raise a fuss and complain about the eggs being cold. This is espe-cially true today, when we know that many modern women are no longer willing to take the time to cook eggs for their hus-band. Constant criticism from a person you're trying hard to please can begin to affect your mind, and people criticized in this way often become depressed.

*No matter how hard we try, we'll never win some people's approval.*

If that husband continuously complains about the way his wife prepares his eggs, and she's living to please him, she may eventually begin to think, "Lord, I don't know how to cook eggs anymore." Deep down inside she should know that she's a master at it, but the con-stant negativity can convince her otherwise.

We must never allow anyone to "mess" with our minds in this way. It may displease this wife initially, but she must come to the point that she can say (lovingly but forceful-ly), "If you 'throw a fit' one more time about the way I cook your eggs, you can cook them yourself." We're called to do what is right—not just what pleases others.

No matter how hard we try, we'll never win some peo-ple's approval. If it's not in their heart to care for us, nothing we can do will change that fact. And if we try to change it by force, we'll end up living in depression and confusion.

That person whose affection you're trying so hard to win may look at you one day and say they don't love you anymore because you're "too fat." Then, after you've gone on a diet, they may decide that you're "too skinny." They may say your hair's "too short" or "too long." If you live your whole life trying to win the affections of a person by pleasing them instead of being true to yourself, you will be most miserable. We must all guard against this evil. Learn to do what is right, and don't worry so much about what others think of it. None of us can afford to let people put us down emotionally.

### Understanding Your Value and Walking in Victory

The problem with people pleasers is that they try too hard, and this turns people off. Rather than winning approval, they usually do just the opposite. In their quest for respect, they lose all respect. When we know within ourselves who we are, that makes all the difference.

There are some cold-blooded people in this world who think nothing of taking advantage of people pleasers and putting them through all sorts of emotional abuse, having discovered their weakness. But we were not designed for such bondage. God created us to be overcomers.

Trying to please everyone around you in order to make yourself feel like you are somebody is a dead-end street. Before you can prove anything to others, you yourself have to know that you are somebody. But once you know that you are somebody, you don't have anything to prove.

I don't have to prove that I'm black. It would be absurd for me to stand up in public places and say,

"Look at me. I've got black skin." I know that I'm black, and when you know who you are, you don't have to prove it to anyone.

For those of us who are in Christ Jesus, we really ought to know who we are. We have the privilege of having the God of the universe living inside of us.

And, as I've noted, we should be able to like who we are. Some people will never grow in life because they don't like or understand who they are. And when you don't like who you are, eventually you will find yourself exhausted, burned out, filled with disillusion, and feeling less secure about yourself than you should.

If you find yourself experiencing these kinds of feelings, or if you're struggling with a need to please people as a result of such feelings, you must change the manner in which you relate to other people. You must resolve, with God's help, to redirect your life and your energy toward becoming a whole and healthy person, one who no longer requires the acceptance and affirmation of others to prove their worth

### Determine If You Are a People Pleaser

Although the knowledge of truth is intended to bring freedom, there are many people who don't want to be free. Some, after discovering their problem, will say to themselves, "Well, I guess I'm just a people pleaser then," and they will continue to live the way they've been living. The goal of discovering the truth about ourselves is to become free and not continue living in bondage.

If you've discovered that you're a people pleaser, why not desire to be free of it? You can be.

In order to walk in freedom from people pleasing, you need to redirect your need to please. Your focus now needs to change.

First, if you've discovered that you are not a people pleaser, you may have another serious problem if you only think about pleasing yourself. There are many selfish people alive today who never give a thought to blessing others. If you fit this description, recognize your problem and work to resolve it. Life is not all about pleasing yourself and never thinking about others. It must be balanced.

As Christians, our desire should always be to please God, and living to please others and living to please God are not one and the same—as some have imagined. If you have felt that pleasing God and pleasing others is the same thing, you must confront this myth with reality. When we learn to please God, we will then know how to effectively please others. So when we have successfully redirected our pleasing process to pleasing God first, everything else will fall into place.

For example, I don't want members of Greater St. Stephen, where I pastor, coming to our Word Explosion Bible Study because they don't want me "going off" on them when they don't attend. I don't want them to attend just because they want to please me, their pastor; I want them to attend because they want to please God by being where He wants them to be when He wants them to be there. It's far better when we do it to please Him and obey His Word. He has said:

*Not forsaking the assembling of ourselves togeth-er, as the manner of some is; but exhorting one another: and so much the more, as ye see the day approaching.*

Hebrews 10:25

Everything else falls in line when our goal is to faith-fully attend church because we know what God has said about it. Our mindset should be: "When my church has some activity that requires my attendance, I must do my best to be there, not forsaking the assembling together, and, as a result, pleasing God." When we please God, others will be pleased, and we will be blessed.

Redirecting our pleasing and allowing our efforts to please God always produces something good. Once I understand what God's will is, I offer my body as a living sacrifice, *"holy and pleasing"* to Him, and I don't worry what men may think of me. What could be more impor-tant than the will of our God?

People pleasers also offer their bodies as a living sacri-fice (sometimes literally), but not to please God. Their sac-rifice is to please people. But when we allow people to con-trol us in this way, we begin to operate outside the will of God. Whatever we do for people must always line up with the will of God. He is the only one we must be concerned about pleasing, so we should never be motivated to do something only because we want the accolades of men.

No matter what I do in life, I want to make sure that I'm pleasing God. That's my ultimate goal. Someone may be blessed by my actions, but I do what I do to please God. I help people, not so that I can go around saying that I helped them, but because I want to please God. And the reason I live to please Him is that He is God, and He has done wonderful things in my life.

Always seek to please God first, and worship none other than Him. This includes our spiritual leaders. I encourage the congregation God has placed me over not to obey me just because they are people pleasers, but because they honor God. I do want them to respect me as a man of God, but I want them to do it because God has commissioned them to. He said:

*Obey them that have the rule over you, and submit yourselves: for they watch for your souls, as they that must give account, that they may do it with joy, and not with grief: for that is unprofitable for you.*

Hebrews 13:17

*Let the elders that rule well be counted worthy of double honour, especially they who labour in the word and doctrine.*

1 Timothy 5:17

I want our church members to be motivated by God's Word, because if their actions are not motivated by His Word, in the moment I displease them in some way, they might refuse to bless me with their love offerings. Even in this, I want them to be motivated by what God has said:

*Thou shalt not muzzle the ox that treadeth out the corn.*

1 Timothy 5:18

Because God tells us to bless the men of God, if our church members are living to please Him, even when they get upset with me they cannot cut off their love offerings. They cannot muzzle this ox because it's not about me; it's about God.

Some of our church members may not understand everything God leads me to do. I don't expect everybody to understand me all the time. That's why God sets leaders in place. If a leader is always on the same level as the congregation, as it relates to the revelation of the vision of where God is taking that congregation, that leader really isn't a leader at all. As a leader, God has to reveal some things to me before He gives them to the congregation, and it may take the congregation a while to catch up. A leader, by definition, has to be out ahead of the pack, knowing the way and leading the way. But if we can all keep our focus on God and work to please Him, together we will see the plan of God come to pass.

*A leader, by definition, has to be out ahead of the pack, knowing the way and leading the way.*

### Developing Healthy Relationships with **God** and with **People**

When we give our all to please others, we're actually engaging in a type of worship toward them, and this is a serious mistake. People pleasers are convinced that this type of behavior is virtuous, but it cannot be. How can it be virtuous when it's done with the unconscious motive of gaining approval and acceptance?

On the other hand, when we live to please God, it is not with the desire to receive something from Him. We do it because we love Him and for no other reason. We do it because of what we've already received from Him, not for some hope of future gain.

When we develop a relationship with someone only for the sake of what we can get from them, that's not healthy. We should be thankful to God for the opportunity to serve others in obedience to Him, nothing else.

It's difficult to work with people effectively if your entire purpose is to get something from them. I am where I am today because I served the church for many years with no hope of personal gain, and I did not do it to please men, but to please God.

This, I believe, is why the former pastor of Greater St. Stephen, Pastor Simpson, felt comfortable with me. He knew that I did not covet his position and would not make any effort to replace him. I knew that God had him in the church for that particular time, and I was just happy to have the privilege of being his assistant.

I worked hard as assistant pastor of the church, and I was grateful to God for allowing me to serve in that position. But I didn't serve for what I could get out of it or just to please others. I served because I loved the Lord and for no other reason.

If we Christians cannot come to an understanding of service without thought of reward, we're in danger of being no different than the world around us. This is why the Bible warns:

*Do not conform any longer to the pattern of this world, but be transformed by the renewing of your mind.*

Romans 12:2, NIV

We cannot afford to get caught up in the way the world does things—walking all over other people and misusing them in an effort to gain superiority and be somebody. We don't have any reason to strive to try to become somebody if we're in relationship with God and our relationships with the people around us are healthy.

When God brings us into relationship with himself, we become somebody automatically. If you're a believer, the moment you were born again you entered into relationship with God as His child. That means a lot.

I'm God's child, and because I'm God's child, certain things will automatically happen in my life. I don't have to try to make them happen; they *will* happen. I don't have to try to be somebody; I *am* somebody in Him.

I am a child of God, and as a child of God, I know that there are certain things that will automatically come my way, and no one can prevent them. Therefore, I don't have to struggle; I can trust God to keep blessing me the way He wants to bless me. And I don't have to rush the process because I understand who I am.

So if I am in God and my relationships to the people around me are healthy, I can relax and be who I am. I have nothing to prove.

The full realization of the benefits God has intended for us comes with time, as we cooperate with the Holy Ghost's efforts to grow us into the people we were meant to be. If you're living according to the will of God and not just to please the people around you, you have to believe that where you are now is where God wants you to be, but that even now He's in the process of moving you to where He wants to you to go in the future.

Some people's efforts at people pleasing indicate a sense of insecurity in their lives. But when we trust the move of God in our lives and we understand who we are in Him, we have no need to try to push somebody else out of the way and attempt to take their place. This is done by people who are very insecure and unconsciously think they're not valuable otherwise.

People who are not team players and who always try to push other people out of the way are most assuredly insecure. They're afraid that if somebody else works with them or assists them, the other person may do a better job and eventually replace them. So they push that person out. They do this, not necessarily because they don't like the people they're working with, but because they have no confidence in themselves.

I have never been the kind of pastor who feels that he can do it all by himself, and I have never been hesitant to work with others, because I know who I am. I prefer to surround myself with people who know what they're doing because I understand that when I do that it can only help me. At the same time, those who work with me can discover their value in the kingdom as they are allowed to use their gifts.

Unfortunately, not every pastor has this same spirit. In some cases, no one ever dares to bring new ideas into a leadership meeting because whenever anyone has tried it, the pastor has accused them of trying to take over. This indicates that the pastor is insecure and doesn't yet understand his own worth. No one can move you out of your position if you're placed there by God, and if you're working with people who have good ideas and only want to help you go to the next level, what harm could possibly result from their ideas? We all need to understand this better.

I've seen far too many one-man and one-woman shows in ministry, in which one person tries to do everything by themselves. People who do that never succeed. They eventually get too many irons in the fire, and because they're hesitant to ask anyone for help, they'll eventually fail. Insecurity, brought on by not knowing who you are, can cause you to do some crazy things.

Know who you are, and work to please God—not people.

### Walk in True Humility and the Assurance of God's Presence

Jesus said very clearly:

*And I will pray the Father, and he shall give you another Comforter, that he may abide with you for ever; even the Spirit of truth; whom the world cannot receive, because it seeth him not, neither knoweth him: but ye know him; for he dwelleth with you, and shall be in you.*

John 14:16-17

This is what God has given to us through the Holy Ghost—*"the Spirit of truth,"* so that we can avoid all insecurity and the need to live to please others. The world cannot understand truth and hates it when we stand up and speak the truth (especially the truth about who Jesus is). It's because they don't have *"the Spirit of truth"* in them. If you mention Jesus, they don't want to hear it because they don't understand what truth is all about.

But we have *"the Spirit of truth"* living inside of us and, because He's inside of us, we're valuable, and we can succeed in life. Stop letting your head hang down, and stop standing in the background acting like you're nobody. False humility is no virtue.

Some think that they're displaying humility when they refuse to use their gifts, but that's not humility. When we stay humble before the Lord, He will direct us and place us where we need to be. But then, if God has given you a gift (to sing, for instance) and you stay in the background, refusing to use your gift, you're not being humble. That's not humility; it's stupidity. God expects us to use the gifts He's given us to bring Him glory and to bless others. Walk in that truth.

Jesus said further:

*I will not leave you comfortless: I will come to you.*

John 14:18

Whatever God has given you to do, you can feel confident in pursuing it—when you understand that He's with you. His presence makes all the difference. You don't need to live to please others.

Let's pretend for a moment that you're walking down the street with Evander Holyfield. Would you have to be concerned with some little chump who walked up to you and said that he was going to "knock your block off"? Not if you have Holyfield standing next to you. Well, as believers, we have the Holy Ghost inside of us, and Jesus has said that He would never leave us without the Comforter.

God is with us, so get rid of all your low self-esteem and stop living to please others. Understand who you are, and don't let the devil "mess" with your mind even a moment longer.

### Refuse to Allow Satan to Limit You

As we have seen, if you let him do it, the devil will have you believing that you're limited because of where you happen to live or because of where you happened to grow up. Again, that's nothing but a trick of the enemy. I know people who came from the ghetto, and they can put to shame some of those who grew up in the wealthiest neighborhoods. Where you go in life depends on what you think about yourself and how much you believe in yourself, not what neighborhood you've come from. That doesn't matter.

Our church has locations in three different parts of greater New Orleans, but no matter which location I preach in, the message is the same. Everybody gets the same preaching, regardless of location. It doesn't matter what neighborhood you've come from; what matters is the fact that you're born again, and you now belong to God. If we can realize this more fully, our success in life will no longer be determined by the circumstances of our birth or where we happened to grow up.

Some are not aware of the fact that the people of Jesus' day had a problem with where He grew up. Even one of His disciples, when he first heard about Jesus being the Messiah, said:

*Can there any good thing come out of Nazareth?*

John 1:46

In the days and weeks to come, Jesus showed everyone that some good could come out of that infamous town, and this is what we must all be willing and able to do. We must show the world what God has done for us and what He can do for them through us—regardless of and in spite of the circumstances of our birth and the environment in which grew up.

Once our minds are renewed by the Holy Ghost, we will begin to understand that we are indeed valuable in God's sight, and we will cease to worry about needing to prove that we are somebody in the sight of others—regardless of where we came from and regardless of the color of our skin. It would be a waste of our time and energy to try to make some people believe it, but as long as we're all right in God's sight, we can make it in life. When you work to please God, people with good sense will see it. And the people who don't have good sense ... well, don't worry about them. Once we get hold of this truth, no one will be able to stop us.

Know who you are in Him today, and start walking in victory. In this way, by examining yourself, you will put to flight *The Enemy Inside Your Mind.*

# CHAPTER 6

# The Spirit of Domination

———»•◦•«———

*When I was a child, I spake as a child, I under-*
*stood as a child, I thought as a child: but when I*
*became a man, I put away childish things.*

1 Corinthians 13:11

There's another area of truth that I feel is necessary for us to examine if we're to discover the whole truth about ourselves. Before you finish reading the book, one of these areas will hit you (if one hasn't hit you already), and it will help you to walk in victory. In this chapter, I would like to deal with the subject of domination. Toward the end of the chapter, you will discover why I have used this particular verse as a text.

Dominators are people who are afraid of losing control, for they derive their identity through what they do and who looks up to them while they're doing it. Therefore they feel the urgent need to dominate everything and everybody around them.

Whether on the job, in the home, or in the church, dominators take their positions so seriously that they begin to operate outside the will of God.

## Characteristics of Dominators

Many times a person's greatest strength, the dominant part of their personality, can become their greatest weakness. So it is with dominators. They are often good leaders, they like the feeling they get by being in charge, and because they live in fear of losing control, they end up using whatever tactics they deem necessary to gain or maintain control. In the process, they become liars and backstabbers, and they will do whatever is necessary to degrade another person so that they can take over.

This is the reason it's so important for us to be careful in whom we confide. Every person who smiles at you is not necessarily on your team. If you share the intimate details of your personal life with someone who turns out to be a dominator, that person could take what you tell them and use it against you. They might use it to get what they want from you, or they might use it to gain power over certain areas of your life.

Typically, dominators are critical and demanding people, and they're bad tempered and easily angered when things don't go their way. Their anger frequently flares, and they use it and the resulting verbal and physical abuse that comes with it as a means of domination over others.

This kind of behavior has become commonplace in our world today, but it's also to be found in the church. I'm sad to say that I see dominating behavior in born-again believers who want power so badly that they operate abusively toward each other.

Another characteristic of dominators is that they always need to be "in the know." This is the reason some people stay on the telephone for hours every day. They're gathering information to be used at the appropriate moment. They just have to have call waiting, caller I.D., three-way calling, and every other conceivable advantage so that they can compile more data for their personal use.

"Guess what I learned today, Child?" they say, when they've called you. "Can I tell you this?" They have every intention of telling you because this is part of their routine.

If you find yourself struggling with always needing to be "in the know" or always using anger to manipulate someone or some situation, you need to carefully examine whether or not you might be a dominator.

## Dominators vs. Non-Dominators

To some degree, all of us have a dominating spirit. It doesn't matter who you are. There are some things you want to be in control of. So what's the difference between dominators and non-dominators? The difference is great, and it lies in the fact that dominators are obsessed with control. They simply have to be in charge (regardless of the circumstances), and they will do anything to assure that they are in charge.

For instance, some people can't ride in another person's car without being in charge. You may be an experienced and cautious driver, but when a dominator gets into the car with you, every time you put on the brakes, you see them putting on the brakes too. They're constantly telling you, "Watch out for this or that." They can't help themselves. They're obsessed.

*...being in power can never really define who you are.*

This may sound like someone you know, or it may even sound like you.

Being in charge, for a dominator, is a matter of survival, and a person who has this spirit struggles with it constantly. Consequently, they live in constant competition with everyone and everything around them. That must be an exhausting way of life.

In order to be free from this spirit, a dominator must first face the reality that even if they could maintain control of everyone and everything in their world, it still wouldn't prove their worth as a person. In other words, being in power can never really define who you are.

Dominators try to make a name for themselves by creating the image of being important. To this end, they employ their many talents, never realizing that they can never prove their self-worth in this way.

### Total Domination Is Impossible

The apostle Paul wrote to the Corinthians:

*We walk by faith, not by sight.*

2 Corinthians 5:07

If we could dominate everything around us, we might be able to walk by sight. But, because we cannot dominate everything around us, we have to walk by faith.

What is faith? The writer of Hebrews answered the question this way:

> *Faith is the substance of things hoped for, the evidence of things not seen.*
>
> Hebrews 11:1

Each of us must accept the fact that we simply cannot dominate everything.

### How to Gain Freedom from a Dominating Spirit

When we come to the point that we can admit that only God has the power to be in control, we free ourselves to release our feeble grasp at domination. In the process, we must let go of our fear of losing the upper hand, and that fear is real and powerful. This underlying fear that causes dominators to dread ever losing domination must be dealt with decisively.

What will people think of you if you no longer have the upper hand? How will people react to you if you're no longer in a position of authority? This harkens back to the need for approval from others, and it is, as I have previously shown, unimportant. Never be trapped into living for the approval of other people. It's only by redirecting your focus from pleasing people to pleasing God that you can live in total freedom.

The dominating spirit, the one that operates in the life of a dominator, is a heavy one, and it almost always adversely affects the personal relationships of the individual who harbors it. If you find yourself always struggling in your relationships with other people, you might want to ask yourself the question, "Am I a dominator?" If you discover that you are, it's not the end of the world. But you will have to be willing to take the necessary steps to be free from that spirit so that you can walk in truth and freedom.

## Domination and Relationships

Over time, any person tires of excessive control, and therefore relationships like these usually sour. Some dominators want to do all your thinking for you, and if you attempt to think for yourself, they may call you "crazy," "foolish," or "stupid." This is just how they talk.

Dominators are convinced that they need to do all the thinking for you because you don't know how to think for yourself. Consequently, they can be very difficult marital partners. They find it nearly impossible to live and let live. Rather, it's usually their way or no way, and they can make life miserable for the person who refuses to go along with them.

Dominators get upset over the smallest detail of life that seems to elude their grasp. For instance, if the telephone rings and someone has dialed a wrong number, they become visibly disturbed. "Who was that?" they yell. When their spouse tells them it was a wrong number, they find that difficult to accept and feel the need to make a big fuss over the matter.

But what can the spouse answer? We can't be in control of wrong numbers, and we have to accept the fact that people sometimes do dial mistakenly. But so what? If someone has dialed a wrong number, that's nothing to get excited about. It's just a wrong number. Why make something more of an occurrence like this than it really is? But a dominator can't seem to leave it alone. They're angry at the whole world.

Having this kind of relationship in marriage is not what God intended, and therefore it's important for us to bind this spirit of domination and get victory over it. This is clearly not of God, and it will cause harm to the relationship sooner or later.

The enemy delights in it. He doesn't care what tactic he uses to destroy intimate relationships and friendships, and this is one that he uses often.

When the spouse of a dominator begins to claim their own space or their own thoughts or feelings, the dominator becomes angry, resentful, and even abusive. This shows what type of spirit we're dealing with here. If this describes you, get rid of this spirit before it destroys you.

### You're the Problem

Rather than point the finger at others today, I want you to take a good look at yourself. Do you allow other people to do their own thinking? Do you let them express themselves? Or do you feel compelled to always express their thoughts for them? Be sure that you're not operating out of a spirit of domination.

In some cases, dominators seem never to recognize why they have problems in their relationships. Unless they're confronted by someone from the outside, how can they know? Unfortunately, many of them avoid sitting down and talking with anyone other than their mate, so they go on assuming that they're right in their way of thinking. This is one of the principal reasons I chose to address this issue here. So take a good look at your own behavior. Examine yourself as you discover the truth through this chapter.

Some people can lie to themselves so successfully that they become convinced that they have every justification in the world for their dominating behavior. If you have this problem, rather than excusing yourself, please be honest and find a way to deal with it.

Those of us who are married must understand that our spouse is not one of our children, and they must never be treated as a child. They're an adult, and they're to be treated as an adult. This means that we give them all due respect.

Although you may be in relationship with them, and marriage partners often make decisions together, there are some decisions that your spouse must make on their own. You cannot make every decision for them, so don't try it.

Your spouse will sometimes make a wrong decision, but even if they end up looking stupid because of some decision they've made, you have to let them make it. There are some things you must allow them to do—even if you don't agree with them.

If you're one of those who fail to give your spouse room to make their own decisions, your marriage will degenerate into nagging, and nobody wants to live in a nagging relationship. Certain freedoms must exist between a husband and wife, or marriage becomes more like a prison sentence than the blessing it was intended to be.

If you catch yourself always nagging your spouse, check yourself to see if you might be a dominator. I even encourage you to sit down with your family and have some frank discussions with them on this issue. In this way, you can make sure that your relationships are healthy ones.

*If you catch yourself always nagging your spouse, check yourself to see if you might be a dominator.*

Please don't go to your spouse and say, "You need to read this book because you have the problem he describes!" If they do have a problem, help them to discover it on their own, as difficult as that may be. This always works best.

I can't know everything that's going on in your home or in your relationships, but thirty years of pastoral service have taught me some important things about domination: (1) There are many people struggling with the issue of domination, especially in regard to their relationships, and (2) When problems occur in their life, such dominators usually blame their problems on something or someone else and fail to acknowledge that the problem may be with them personally.

If you happen to be the one causing the problems in your marriage, let me assure you that you don't have to nag in order to make things work. You don't have to make decisions for other people. As adults, they can make their own decisions.

There are some people who actually feel that they even have to tell their spouse how to dress. It may be appropriate to tell them occasionally that you don't like how they've dressed, and if you do it in the right way, they may receive your criticism and change. But if you insist on harping constantly on this subject, it will surely put a strain on your relationship. Give your spouse the freedom to wear what they want to wear.

There are cases in which people dress inappropriately. Not everyone has impeccable taste in clothing. If this is true of your spouse, and you go out and two or three other people tell your spouse that what they have on doesn't look good, then you're position is justified. But, even if your spouse is not color coordinated, if you're constantly nagging them about it, they'll eventually begin to dismiss out of hand your criticisms as unworthy of serious consideration.

### Make Your Confession Today

There are many other situations in which dominators insist on carrying the load. They're forever trying to "straighten things out." Then, when they can't get things straightened out as they had hoped, they become angry. Things are out of their power, and this frightens them terribly.

Every dominator must come to the point that they're ready and willing to change their false assumptions.

They must confront their false beliefs and identify them as being false. They must admit to themselves that they have a problem and stop justifying their wrong behavior. Then they can begin to make the necessary changes.

The Bible speaks to us of growing up. It says:

*When I was a child, I spake as a child, I understood as a child, I thought as a child: but when I became a man, I put away childish things.*

1 Corinthians 13:11

It is a lie that if we lose control something terrible will happen. Therefore, we must renounce our childish ways and all attempts at dominating others, and we must yield all control of our lives to the Lord, our God.

There was probably a point in your life where you had to stand up and let people know who you were. If you didn't, they would have walked all over you. Now that you're grown, however, those tactics are no longer necessary. Children have a need to make their identity known, but that need should not become a continuous struggle that dominates the rest of life.

This is an area where many young people go wrong. They think they have to spend the rest of their lives fighting to prove who they are. But there must come a point in your life when *you* know who you are, and then you won't have to prove it over and over again to others.

With some, this struggle for identity goes on long into their adult life. When I mentioned publicly that I would retire after a certain age from pastoring, other pastors called me to ask, "What will you do then?" This thought seemed inconceivable to them.

"I'm afraid to retire from pastoring," they admitted, "for fear I'll have nothing to do." But being retired from pastoring didn't frighten me at all, and it still doesn't. I know that if I'm no longer pastoring Greater St. Stephen, I'll still be somebody. There are many things to be accomplished in this world—more than enough to go around.

If we know who we are, we have no psychological need for domination, and our self-worth is not derived from a position or a title, but from what God has done in our lives. This is a much healthier position to take.

I've noticed that some people hold on to a position because they're afraid that if they don't continue working in that position, when they die, nobody will come to their funeral. If they retire, they worry, "Not enough people will know or remember who I was." What they don't seem to realize is that they won't be there to know who comes or doesn't come to their funeral.

But that's just like dominators. They want a big funeral, and if they lose power or their position, they feel they won't have it. They seem to be worried about not appearing to be in power—even after they are deceased. What a terrible way to live!

### *The Act of Relinquishing Power to God Once and for All*

The need to dominate other people and situations is a heavy burden to carry. What we must do is face the reality that God is in control. Once you get to the level where you truly understand that He's in control, you'll no longer feel the need to dominate everything and everyone around you.

There are many things that I want to see done in the ministry of Greater St. Stephen where I pastor, but I realize that God has to be in control. I would rather allow Him to convict people through His Word, as opposed to using fleshly means of motivating them. His way works so much better. I'd rather preach and teach the Word of God concerning what the congregation should be doing, instead of trying to *make* them do what I want them to do out of fear. I let God have control, and the result is always as it should be.

You need to do this same thing in your situation. It doesn't matter what you're facing in your life, I dare you to turn it over to the Lord. Tell Him about it, and then let Him have control of the situation. He knows how to fix your problem, and He can do it much better than you could by becoming frustrated and resorting to abusive language and violence against others.

The fact that you can't dominate everything is what people have been trying to tell as you experienced friction in your relationships. You haven't wanted to hear it, but now you must hear it. You're not in control; God is. So give Him total power over all things.

If you want to go to the next level, you must confess that it's His world, and as His child, you can trust Him to run it. Do you trust Him? Can you turn everything over to Him?

You haven't trusted other people and have felt many times that they could do nothing right, so can you trust God? Are you so much in charge that you can't trust even

Him when He says that He will open doors of opportunity for you? Can you trust Him enough to believe that He will do what He said He would do? Or will you insist on continuing to be the master of your own fate?

I will touch on trust a little more toward the end of the chapter. Suffice it to say at this point that many people who have had the problem of dominating others find it difficult to finally let go and let God take charge of their lives and everyone and everything in it. This is one reason some don't tithe. They know what God has said about tithing, but they continue to look at their own lack and feel that if they tithe they won't be able to make ends meet. They choose to maintain power and try to make their existing finances stretch to meet every need, rather than obeying God in the tithe and trusting Him to make the ninety percent go further.

*God is totally trustworthy, so it's time that you begin to trust Him.*

But God is totally trustworthy, so it's time that you begin to trust Him. He is more than able to meet every one of your needs. He has all power, and He has promised to always be there for you. I believe with all my heart that He will be. He declared in His Word:

*I will never leave thee, nor forsake thee.*

Hebrews 13:5

We have this promise from the God of the universe, the Almighty, that He will be there for us when we need Him. So what are you worried about? Let God be in charge of every situation and every person in your life, and you keep your focus on examining yourself. That's a full-time job in itself.

I know that some of you are awesome individuals, and you can seemingly take care of yourself and fifty other people at the same time. But I think if you really work on yourself and let others do the same, you'll be a lot more productive.

Because God has said that He will be with us, we don't have to worry about being in charge. Rather than falsely believing that we're the masters of our own fate, we must let go of our need for constant control. Let God be God in the world, in our own lives, and in the lives of those around us.

It's time for you to be happy and not be burdened with the weight of trying to be in charge in areas in which you were never intended to have control. But the only thing that can bring on this change is for you to change. You can talk about changing all you want to, but if you don't make an effort to change, there will be no change.

I pray that my sharing this word of God with you in these pages has spoken to you. If it fits you, if it hits you where you're living, please take it to heart. Become willing to take a good look at yourself and to make whatever changes are necessary to correct your problem.

Allowing God to control everything about your life is true liberty. Insisting on being in charge is a guise that can never satisfy.

## Domination and Ministry

If you've been a dominator, you must recognize that your need to be in charge has been doing great damage to your relationships. And if you're a leader, it has been limiting your effectiveness.

I've been CEO of Greater St. Stephen Ministries for many years now, but our employees can tell you that I never walk through the office building like I'm someone important, checking out every office. I don't have the need to do that because I know that I'm the boss. No one has to tell me that I'm the CEO, and I have no need to prove it to anyone. This allows me to relax and let everyone do their job.

When you know who you are, you don't have to make people's lives miserable just to prove a point. You don't have to strive constantly to impress others. Your goal is not to impress people, but to impress God. Your prayer should be:

*Lord, I want You to see what I'm doing, and I want You to see that I'm doing it for Your glory, for Your honor, and for Your praise.*

When we can get that thought into our spirits, life around us will suddenly become beautiful.

When I die, I don't want people to be relieved and say, "I'm glad he's gone!" The only way I can avoid a sad end like that is to deal honestly with myself and walk in truth. If I fail to do that, I can do irreparable harm to my relationships.

Other people have the right to their own space and freedom and the right to choose to be who they want to be. We can encourage them, and we can talk to them about what we see God doing in their lives, and we can pray for them. But that's as far as we can go.

All of us should be involved in encouraging others. As a pastor, I certainly am. But God has not assigned any of us to serve as the FBI in anybody's daily life.

Think about it. God has given us many freedoms. He could have struck us down every time we did something wrong in life, but He didn't do that. Instead, He gives us the right to be free moral agents, to live as we choose to live. He could have been "all over us" every time we "messed up," but He chose to give us the liberty to make our own choices.

If God wanted to, He could have cameras located everywhere we go to expose everything we do. If He wanted to, He could allow other people to watch us at all times. He could do that, but He doesn't.

When we turn the lights out and do whatever it is that we do, there are no cameras there to record it, because God has given us the right to choose. And if God gives us this right to choose, why do we think we have to serve as god in somebody else's life and control everything about them? A dominating spirit is not from God, and it is not His will that we live in this way or cause others to live in this way.

### Understanding the Need for Balance

There is always a need for balance in every teaching. Some people go too far to the left, and others go too far to the right. Get the balance.

I'm not saying that we should not be concerned for others. We should. I'm not saying that we should not try to help others. We should. I'm not saying that we should not give others advice. We should. What I'm talking about here in this chapter is an over-dominating spirit.

I'm not asking you to adopt the attitude: "Good! I'm not telling anybody anything else as long as I live." We need to be able to communicate with other people about their needs and to help them. That's what maturity is all about. I'm assuming that you're spiritual enough to know that I am dealing here with balance as it relates to how we should live and how we should treat one another, and I'm trying to help someone not to overdo it. We must allow people to have their own opinions, and we must allow them to make their own decisions in life.

We would all probably have to admit that we have been guilty of stifling others to some degree or another. I know that I have. When I married, my wife was just twenty-two years old, and because I was older, I felt that I had to tell her many things. She was okay with this. But when some years had gone by and I still had the same attitude, she said to me one day, "Look, Honey, I'm twenty-eight now." She meant that she no longer needed me to tell her the things I had told her at twenty-two. There comes a time when you can't keep treating people like they're children.

The biblical doctrine of submission is often taken out of context and misused. We must be able to submit to one another as God has instructed us to, but when talking about submission, some leave out the scriptures that speak to us of the *"due benevolence,"* the respect, and the honor that each mate must have for the other:

*Let the husband render unto the wife due benevo-
lence: and likewise also the wife unto the husband.*

1 Corinthians 7:3

*Likewise, ye husbands, dwell with them according
to knowledge, giving honour unto the wife, as unto
the weaker vessel, and as being heirs together of the
grace of life; that your prayers be not hindered.*

1 Peter 3:7

As we noted earlier, married couples must be willing
to respect their mate as their mate, never treating them
like a daughter or son, a hired hand, or an underling, but
as a spouse deserves to be treated. This is a part of the
process of submission that is often overlooked in our
teachings. Married couples must realize that their spouse
is a special gift from God to them, and then they must
treat them accordingly.

The need for mutual respect goes far beyond the marriage relationship. In leadership, we must treat each person
under us as a man or woman befitting dignity and honor.

When you have been elevated to a position of leadership, never do as some, and get a big head just because
you now have a title. I've literally seen people change
overnight when they were appointed to a position. This
is very sad.

There is nothing else, in my experience, that can
affect a person quite like gaining a position. I've seen it
in my local church ministry and also in the international
fellowship over which I preside. And those who are
appointed to the highest positions are sometimes the

most guilty of allowing pride to creep in and cause them to become dominating.

If you're chosen to serve in the church, demonstrate that you can handle what God has given to you, and allow the people under you to experience things for themselves. Refuse to use anger and intimidation as a means for dominating them. This is self-defeating behavior wherever it occurs. If you will search the Scriptures for direction, God will change your self-defeating behavior.

### Search the Scriptures

If you, as is common with dominators, still fail to recognize that the problems you face in life originate from within you, listen to the words of Paul in his letter to the Romans:

> For I say, through the grace given unto me, to every man that is among you, not to think of himself more highly than he ought to think; but to think soberly, according as God hath dealt to every man the measure of faith.
>
> Romans 12:3

Paul knew that grace had been bestowed upon him. He was gifted and he was anointed. At the same time, he knew that he had killed many Christians. Therefore, he knew that it was nothing but the grace of God that had brought him to this current level of spiritual service, and he had to be careful not to think of himself more highly than he should.

This recognition is often missing in dominating people. They have no trace of humility. A good dose of humility can very quickly change the attitude of any dominator.

Dominators tend to have an inflated concept of themselves, but once they realize that they're nothing and God is everything, and they begin to relinquish control to Him, it makes all the difference in the world.

If you've been a dominator, recognize your sinful pride today and let God deal with it. Then learn total submission to Him and His will.

### Learn to Trust

This strikes at the very heart of the dominator's primary issue—distrust. Dominators, as we have noted, try to dominate in areas where they lack trust. If they trusted God in that situation, they wouldn't feel the need to always be in charge. Having trust allows one to rest.

I don't have to follow my wife all over town, because I trust her. It's when a person doesn't trust that they feel the need for constant control. So deal with the issue of trust, and your need to dominate will diminish.

Trust is important in our relationship to the Lord, but it is also vital to every other relationship. If you cannot trust, you cannot rest.

If I were not able to trust someone to fill my pulpit when I was out of town, I could never go away. And some pastors nearly kill themselves because they can't trust anyone to help them. They never delegate authority, and, consequently, they never have much help.

The simple fact is that we gain our personhood by relinquishing it. When we submit to God and trust Him, that's when we really become somebody. Search your heart today and allow God to reveal to you anything in you that may be hindering your walk with Him. Then begin to walk in truth and freedom as it relates to the area of control.

It is God's desire to take us all *"from glory to glory"* (2 Corinthians 3:18), and that requires that we be willing to change. Let God change you today. In this way, by calling out a dominating spirit, you will put to flight *The Enemy Inside Your Mind.*

# CHAPTER 7

# "I Have Needs"

———·•·———

*And my God will meet all your needs according to his glorious riches in Christ Jesus.*

Philippians 4:19, NIV

When people have a need, they will seek to meet it, either consciously or unconsciously. This is the reason it is so important for us to make sure we're operating under the power of God. If not, we might seek to fulfill our needs any possible way.

For example, you may have a need to be told occasionally that you look nice, but the one you're in relationship with never tells you. As a result, you may become vulnerable to some other person who sees you and says, "Wow! You look great today!" Constantly hearing the compliments of this other person could eventually put you in a compromising position, as you attempt to get your need for appreciation satisfied. There's nothing wrong with receiving appreciation from others—as long as we receive it from the right people and in the right way.

We must also realize that sometimes people will not appreciate us. Since being appreciated is a basic human need, you may ask, "If other people don't appreciate me, how can I be appreciated?" The answer is that you must come to appreciate yourself. Every day, when I wake up, I take time to appreciate who I am. I thank God for who I am. By doing this, I avoid allowing any controlling force from outside to define me. I never become dependent on other people defining my self-worth. That control has to come from within.

This does not in any way negate our need to be appreciated by others. This is a real need. Stop fooling yourself by saying, "I don't need confirmation of worth or a sense of belonging." Yes you do, and you must recognize it. There's something on the inside of each of us that causes us to desire these things. Whether you have to give it to yourself or it comes from another person, we all like to be appreciated. There's nothing wrong with getting appreciation from others—as long as you understand that appreciation must begin on the inside.

### Identifying Your Needs and Having Them Met Properly

Examining yourself requires you to recognize that you have legitimate needs that must be met, and you must also know how to identify those needs and to know the legitimate from the illegitimate.

"Illegitimate needs?" Yes, some needs are not legitimate. Some people, for instance, are constantly seeking validation. That's not a legitimate need. What do you really need?

There are some weaknesses in your life that you need to work on in order to become a better person, and you may be reaching out to somebody else to meet a need that you can meet on your own. So those are not legitimate needs either.

*Improper motivation often leads to self-deception.*

There are people who become upset with everyone around them if they have on a new dress or a new suit, and no one notices. To their way of thinking, that's a very real need. But it's an illegitimate need. Aside from the desired and deserved attentions of a devoted spouse, a person cannot always expect to be the center of attention with everyone around them. Focus on what your legitimate needs are, and then seek to have those needs met.

Once you've identified your legitimate needs, the next crucial issue is: how do you go about getting those needs met? This is an area that requires caution. Be careful about how you get even legitimate needs met.

Improper motivation often leads to self-deception. We can believe that we're genuinely concerned with meeting the needs of those with whom we are in relationship, when, in reality, what drives us is something very different. Sometimes we're not really trying to help the other person, as we believe. We're really trying to satisfy our illegitimate need to show how great we are.

### God Has Promised to Meet Our Every Need

When I talk about God's ability to meet our needs, I'm actually talking about His unconditional love for us. People never operate in unconditional love. We can act like we operate in unconditional love, but there are always some conditions that we just won't tolerate. Jesus, on the other hand, loves us just as we are—even with all of our mistakes. With people, it's "three strikes and you're out," but with God it's unconditional love. His love has no limitations whatsoever.

This is one of the reasons we should love the Lord— because He's always willing to meet our needs. That's His promise, so my needs can be met, and although I may be looking for them to be met somewhere else, God is the one who supplies all my needs. This is why those of us who are saved and know the Lord ought to be the happiest people in the world and not the most depressed. I can understand people without God being depressed and tired, but not Christians. We have the One who supplies all our needs.

Christians should never be found singing, "I'm tired and I'm weary." As a Christian, you can't encourage anyone if you're always talking about how tired you are on this journey through life. Even the U.S. Army tries to make what they do exciting to those who are considering enlistment. How can we be less excited about serving the Lord when He's promised to meet our every need? That's exciting!

As we noted in an earlier chapter, you're a part of *"a chosen generation"* and *"a royal priesthood"* (1 Peter 2:9). The apostle Peter was talking about you. No matter how much or how little money you have in your pocket or your bank account right now, you're a part of this promise. Begin to understand this and let it become your reality.

Give up your lies and let truth reign in your life. You will never come to like yourself until you come to terms with God's reality (His Word) and get wrapped up in the One who is greater than your negative self-image. His name is Jesus, and He loves you with an everlasting love.

### Dealing with the Reality of Your Needs

So what is the reality when it comes to your needs? Be honest.

The first reality regarding your needs is that they're important. If you still have a hard time believing this, you must change your beliefs. Your needs are important, so don't keep denying the fact that they are, and don't allow yourself to think that you're a weak person if you acknowledge that you have needs. Even strong people have needs.

The second reality regarding your needs is that they must be met. The only valid reason for denying your needs is to help further the kingdom of God. Let me explain.

God sometimes can and will change your entire agenda and redefine your needs when it comes to expanding His kingdom. The kingdom of God is simply God's way of doing things, and in kingdom building, His needs always take precedence over our own. If you deny satisfying your immediate needs for the sake of meeting God's needs, you'll enjoy it, and you'll be blessed. The reason you'll enjoy it is that you'll be doing what He wants you to do. This means that your needs will ultimately be met because whenever you do what God wants you to do, He will supply all your needs.

When I help others and work to build the kingdom of God, denying my own needs temporarily in the process, I always make sure that I'm clearly hearing what God is saying. I want to operate in the kingdom of God, according to His way of doing things. When I do that, I never have to be concerned that my own needs will go unmet. When I operate according to God's way of doing things and effectively meet the needs of others, He always meets my needs in return.

Denying or neglecting one's needs for any reason other than expanding the kingdom of God, as led by the Holy Ghost, is dangerous, and it will not deliver the sense of self-worth you're reaching for. Find the balance.

### Knowing Your Self-Worth in Relationship to Having Your Needs Met

It doesn't matter what anybody has told you; you are somebody. You simply must know that. As we have seen, the destruction of your sense of self-worth may have begun in your childhood, with parents telling you that you were "nothing" or through the uncaring and unfeeling negative reinforcement of some other trusted adult. But regardless of what you were taught in your childhood, you must now come to know your true self-worth. You're valuable to God, and that's all that matters.

Why do I keep returning to this subject over and over again? It's because God has led me to emphasize these truths to raise your self-worth. Far too many have not yet realized just how important they are to Him. When you're in Him, and you come to realize just who you are in Him, your self-worth and your self-esteem will rise. I want to see men and women of God walking and talking like the people they really are.

When the self-worth of any given individual rises, that person will start to do those things that are right for themselves and necessary for them to be blessed and prosper. And when your self-worth goes up, you begin to take pride in your surroundings. If some new carpet is needed at the church where you attend, you may notice it one day and decide to bless the church with some new carpet. When your self-worth is where it needs to be, you take pride in everything with which you are involved. If every Christian could operate in this way, it would quickly change our entire world.

I can sometimes look at people and determine their sense of self-worth just by how they maintain their automobiles. The cars don't have to be new. Just because you have an older model does not mean that it has to be the most ragged car on the street. I have a 1957 model (which means that it will soon be a fifty-year-old car), but it looks good. I keep it looking good because I want it to look good. Maintaining the quality of life around you is part of understanding who you are and in taking pride in who you are.

Some people seem to always have the worst-looking house on the block. But that's not necessary, and it doesn't honor God.

As an African-American, it's sad for me to say, but sometimes I automatically know when I'm entering an African-American neighborhood. The houses are not as well maintained, and the neighborhood is generally messy. This is because many African-Americans have not yet learned to take pride in themselves. They're too busy continuing to blame all their failures on "white folks." Well, it wasn't any "white folks" who came in and made a mess of that neighborhood. It's the responsibility of each of us to take pride in ourselves and in everything that pertains to us—whatever it happens to be.

When I moved to New Orleans many years ago, I came to the city very humbly, with just one suit. Within a short time, doors began to open for me to share the Word of God, and before I knew it, I was preaching several days out of every week. Since I only had one suit, I had to find a dry cleaners that could clean my suit quickly and get it back to me the same day. I had to have it cleaned nearly every day.

I would approach the counter and ask, "Can you get this done for me this afternoon?" And if they couldn't, I had to find another place that could. Until I was able to buy other clothes, I had to keep that one suit in good condition, and I did it because of my sense of who I was and why God had sent me to the city of New Orleans. This holds true whether you have one suit or ten.

Take a look at things around you, and if they're not right, put them right. Take pride in what's yours. If you don't appreciate what you already have, how can God give you more? And if you don't keep it neat and clean, who will?

## Expecting Others to Respect Your Needs

Reality demands that you become attentive to your needs and also that you come to terms with the truth that it's proper to expect others to respect your needs as well. You don't need to be around people who have no respect for your needs. If the people you associate with don't respect you and are constantly calling you a fool or any other derogatory name, maybe you need to change who you're "hanging" with.

You must make the people around you understand that you expect to be respected and that there are things you require of those with whom you associate. If you don't ask for anything, you won't receive anything, as the Scriptures so aptly declare:

*Ye have not, because ye ask not.*

James 4:2

One of the surest ways to destroy a relationship and perpetuate your own self-rejection is for you to do all the giving in that relationship, while asking for nothing in return. Some of you, because your self-worth is so low and you don't want to cause trouble in the relationship, do everything for others and ask for nothing in return. This is not right. You can rid yourself of this behavior by learning to like who you are, recognizing your legitimate needs, and expecting others to respect them as well.

Something is seriously wrong with a marriage relationship when there is a lazy man lying around the house refusing to work and a wife who never confronts him about it because she's "afraid to bother him." What is he there for anyway? Surely women can't be that desperate.

But that's what it looks like when they're "afraid to rock the boat."

Because they don't want their mate to get upset with them, they leave the issue alone, but if you ask nothing, then you'll get nothing in return. You'll move a lot closer to getting your needs met if and when you start communicating those needs and your expectations concerning them to the interested party.

This can be a difficult process, especially at first, and I would not be one to say that it will always be easy. But how can you ever expect to have your needs met if you fail to demand equal consideration in your relationships?

### Effective Communication—the Key to Getting Your Needs Met

It is possible to communicate your needs in such a manner that your fair share will be received. You must use wisdom in doing this, but if you think that keeping silence is a better way to get respect, you will have a miserable relationship.

When people come to me for counseling, I often have to grit my teeth and bear it while they vent their frustrations about all of their spouse's failures. Then, before they leave my office, they say, "Pastor, please don't tell them what I said."

This is crazy. Someone has to tell your spouse how you feel, and that someone should be you. If you find yourself functioning this way—venting your frustrations to others but never communicating your concerns with your husband or wife—I have a question for you: Just how long will you continue to be miserable?

It's amazing how many actually begin their counseling sessions in this way: "Pastor, I want to tell you something about my spouse, but I must ask you not to tell them I said it." If you continue saying nothing about the problem, will it somehow just cure itself? That's not going to happen. If anything is to change in your situation, you must abandon your false beliefs and accept the truth. And the truth is that if you don't change your behavior, there will be no meaningful change in your relationship.

People can have respect for you based only on the way you behave. They have no other way to judge you. Sometimes a man walks all over a good woman who tries as hard as she can to please him. Then, when he finds a woman who stands up to him, he's fine with that and stays with her. The point is that there must be some kind of verbal exchange in which your expectations, needs, and concerns are effectively presented. If this is not done, you cannot blame anyone but yourself for the failure of your marriage.

This teaching is important for those who are already married, and it is also important to single people who are beginning to develop relationships. Single person, you need to understand that learning to identify and communicate your needs to a future spouse is of vital importance. If you have been non-communicative like so many others, change your behavior, and do it today. Reject the false belief that silence will resolve any problem.

People cannot automatically know what you need from them. How can they know unless you tell them? They can't read your mind. You cannot afford to assume that anyone will have such magical powers. If you have not communicated your need, don't blame them for not knowing it.

If you need some space, don't go around to everybody else saying, "They won't give me any space." Tell your spouse that you need some space and make sure they understand that asking for more space doesn't mean you don't love them anymore.

*If you go around for the rest of your life refusing to speak out for yourself, you will be a miserable person.*

All of us need our space. If you're following your spouse from room to room, never allowing them to be alone, that's not good. Give them some space.

If you go around for the rest of your life refusing to speak out for yourself, you will be a miserable person. "I know that they know," some insist. Well, how do they know, if you haven't told them? Is this the way you want to live the rest of your life? If so, it won't be anyone's fault but your own.

Lack of communication is a terrible evil. It opens all sorts of doors for the devil to enter. Each of us must accept personal responsibility for informing others of our wants and desires, and holding it in is never a virtue.

### Communicate an Intolerance for Abuse

Each of us must communicate an intolerance for abuse. You're the only one who can decide that you will no longer allow others to use and abuse you. You can have all the counseling sessions you want, but you still have to make that decision, and then you have to communicate it to the potential abuser.

If you're being physically abused, there must come a point in your life when your self-worth rises to meet the occasion. You must say, "You've hit me for the last time. I don't need anyone that badly. I was making it before I met you, and I can make it without you again."

And when you say it, you have to mean it. You cannot relent the next time he hits you. "I didn't mean it," many women say, as if they had done something wrong. But the proper response is this: "I told you I would be leaving if you ever hit me again. Good-bye!"

Why is that proper? Because your body is the temple of the Holy Ghost, not a punching bag. If you know your self-worth, you will never tolerate that kind of abuse.

Many women insist, "I'm staying for the children's sake," but if you remain in an abusive relationship, you're allowing your children to grow under that influence. As they grow up, they will be confused, and when they marry, they will think that physical abuse is the right way to handle things in a marriage relationship.

So stop using your children as an excuse, and start dealing with the reality of your situation. As you come to know the truth about yourself, it will make you free.

We blame many of our problems on others, but all the while we have the power to make choices and communicate those choices about what we will and will not tolerate. You know what you want and what you need, so make sure that you clearly and specifically communicate those expectations.

### The Power of Honest Discourse

Sharing your needs with others is never done for the purpose of either pleasing or controlling. You're simply being honest with your mate, and since words spoken in honesty have such sincerity about them that people can recognize when you're being honest, your words will have an impact.

Stop holding in your desires. Learning to effectively express your needs is a part of the maturing process in every relationship. Get on with it.

If your husband always goes on trips without you, and you want to go with him, at some point you need to tell him that fact: "Honey, I would like to go with you on one of your trips." Don't take for granted that he knows you want to go. Communicate your desire.

By doing this, you're taking the risk that an argument will ensue. He may not want you to go—for whatever reason. But unless you have communicated your desire, the ball is always in your court. When you know who you are, and you learn to communicate with your spouse openly and honestly, there will eventually be a positive response.

Our failure to communicate is often due to our fear of rejection, but being willing to face rejection is a part of the maturing process. Growing up means that you know how to hear "no" sometimes. Rejection is not the end of the world for a mature person. If they know who they are, they can handle rejection and go forward without difficulty.

If a wife is overworked and needs her husband's help with the household chores, there's nothing wrong with asking him to help with the dishes. She needs to express that need instead of going around the house mumbling and complaining to herself. The worst he can do is say no.

"You never help me with the dishes!" some say in the heat of an argument. But did they ask him to do it? Was he aware of the need? If he refused, that's one thing, but if he didn't know the need, that's inexcusable.

"I have to do all the cooking, wash the dishes, put the clothes in the washing machine and dryer, take clothes to the dry-cleaners, and take the kids to school, and he never lifts a finger to help me." A litany much like this is often heard when nerves are frazzled, but did you ask him? Does he know that you want his help? Don't take it for granted. If you know who you are, you'll not be afraid or hesitant to speak your mind—whether people around you like it or not.

In my work as a pastor, there are sermons that I'm compelled to preach that I know some of my members would rather not hear. Still, I have to preach them. They need to be preached, and I can't be intimidated by what people like or don't like. I have to do what's right, and I can do that because I'm confident in myself. The same is true of our daily communications.

Another concern that needs to be communicated between spouses is the need to spend quality time together. In our modern world, each one has such a hectic schedule that it's very easy to get to the place that we're not spending enough time with each other. This is dangerous, and it's not fun, and that fact must be communicated.

"Honey, I need to spend more time with you." If this is communicated in the right way, it will usually find a very positive response.

*Every communication must be a two-way street.*

———

Learn *how* to approach your spouse about any need. "I'm sick of this, and things have got to change around here," is definitely the wrong approach. Be sweet. Being busy is no one's fault. It happens to us all. Agree to spend more time with each other, and then work to make available the time necessary to do it.

Many spouses let all of their frustrations build up inside of them, and then, when they've gone to bed together at night, it all suddenly comes out. That's a serious mistake. Get it out into the open, and deal with it before it does you serious damage. And, late at night, when you're both tired and you should be thinking of intimate moments together, is no time to address such issues.

Your need may be simply to have your spouse listen to you. That's a very legitimate need, but it won't be resolved just by your getting upset. Communicate your feelings to your mate in a positive and loving way.

Every communication must be a two-way street. In many relationships, one of the spouses does all the talking, and the other has no opportunity. When I experience this in counseling sessions, I sometimes have to say, "Do you ever shut up and give your spouse a chance to talk?" A proper conversation is never one-sided.

If someone cares for you, the very least they can do is to listen to your opinion. They may not agree with what you're saying, and you will almost certainly have disagreements, but that's okay. Never maintain silence just because you think there will be a disagreement.

Disagreements are fairly normal in any relationship. Two people cannot agree on everything. After all, they are individuals, each with a mind of their own. Take the risk, and if your disagreement is sharp, you may sometimes have to agree to disagree. That's not the end of the world. Everyone has a right to their own opinion—even in marriage.

I've seen marriages that fell apart because the husband and wife never talked about their differences. So if you're afraid to confront your spouse because you think they might walk out on you, think again. Not talking presents a greater risk than talking. A lack of communication is always worse than a disagreement.

### Avoiding Angry Exchanges

Even when disagreements do arise, avoid angry exchanges. Instead, express your concerns in a kind and loving way. If you don't like the way your spouse raises their voice at you, don't express that fact to them in a raised voice.

Never belittle or demean your spouse. Loving conversations always work best. Although your spouse may not immediately respond favorably to your expression of concern, if they love you, over time, they will come to understand what you're trying to say to them—if you say it to them in the right way.

Always remember the scriptural admonition:

*Whatsoever a man soweth, that shall he also reap.*

Galatians 6:7

This goes for a woman too. If you are insulting and degrading in the way you address your spouse, what do you expect in return? If you treat your mate like a moron, how do you expect them to respond? You will always reap what you sow.

Learn to argue intelligently. If you do it any other way, you are revealing your own weakness. If you can't carry on an intelligent argument, and you have to look for a crutch, it shows that you're not being honest and forth-right. If you hit someone during a disagreement, it shows that you don't have the maturity necessary for intelligent discussion. You're little better than animals butting heads.

If you feel that you always have to resort to curses in any serious discussion, it shows that you have run out of intelligent words with which to express yourself. That does-n't speak very well of you, does it. Don't be surprised if your mate looks you in the eye and declares, "Well, I see that you've run out of intelligence and resorted to curses!" And if you did it, you deserve that response.

The Bible admonishes us to *"get understanding"*:

*Wisdom is the principal thing; therefore get wisdom: and with all thy getting get understanding.*

Proverbs 4:7

Cursing each other out is not the way to *"get understanding."* Don't act so ignorant. If you or your spouse need

132

time to calm down, suggest it. Say, "I'm willing to discuss this with you, but only after we've both calmed down."

I don't live on Fantasy Island, and I know that some people will not respond well to such a suggestion. "Calm down?" they will demand. "What do you mean, calm down?"

But if you're sure of who you are and not fearful of communicating with your spouse, you'll find a way to calm down the rhetoric so that you can have a decent conversation. Marital disputes can get very heated, and you can either help or hurt the situation. If you insist on always having the last word, and that last word is biting and sharp, you will only escalate matters.

When some people say that they will discuss the matter at a later time, the problem is that they never do. If you say this, mean it, and stick with your intention to stop the shouting and calm things down.

"Oh, no you don't!" one mate may say. "I've got one more thing that has to be said right now!" But this usually just starts up the whole argument all over again. Hold your temper and allow things to cool down. Then you can discuss the matter intelligently.

You must have a clear strategy, even when having a heated conversation, because you don't want things to escalate out of control. You can't risk ending the relationship because the two of you can't communicate properly.

### Will You Pass on a Blessing or a Curse?

My wife and I have had a great marriage now for almost thirty years, but we've had to learn a lot to make it successful. I was determined from the start for it to be a marriage that would speak to our children. They watch us, you know, and I wanted them to have good role models for their own marriages.

*None of us lives only unto ourselves. What we do affects many others around us.*

None of us lives only unto ourselves. What we do affects many others around us. It's selfish not to care about what happens to our children. If we don't care about anybody but ourselves, then there's no reason to make sure that our lives are in order. But if we want to pass on a good example for our children to follow, we need to be more careful.

You can either curse your children or bless them, and every good parent wants to learn how to bless their children. Therefore, we must learn, not only how to successfully deal with marriage, but also how to successfully deal with life in general.

What you do on a daily basis speaks louder than words. How do you handle the situations life sends your way? Does your blood pressure go up? Or do you refuse to get upset? If you learn to take authority over the forces at work in the world around you, your children will learn from that and be able to experience victory in their lives as well.

As you learn to effectively communicate your needs to each other and to your children, they're learning how to handle the communication of needs to their own future spouses and children. In this way, you are actually blessing future generations.

### Never Allowing Others to Define You

In all of this discussion about communicating needs, I have never suggested that you tell a spouse or a prospective spouse, "I need you to love me," or "I need you to respect me as a person." This would be reaching out for something that you should already have. If a person feels that you need their acceptance because you don't love yourself enough to realize that you're important, it could open the door for them to take advantage of you. You may need a person's respect, but you should never have to be on your knees pleading for it.

"I need you to love me," is not a proper plea. If you're asking someone to love you, maybe you need to learn to love yourself first. Then others will love you too. But you cannot force someone to love you.

When I'm counseling any troubled couple, the first question I ask them is if they still love each other. If that all-important foundation is missing, I would be wasting my time talking with them about other issues. Any marriage that is devoid of love will not last long.

If someone doesn't love you, all of your begging for their love will not change that fact. Try as you might, you simply cannot force them to love you.

You should be able to say to your spouse, "These are the things that I would like to see happen in our marriage," but don't look to them for personal validation. Don't expect them to convince you that you're a person of worth. If you need someone to tell you that you're valuable, then you've given that person the power to define you, and that's dangerous. They might get mad at you someday and call you a dog or something even worse, and then you would identify yourself the way they see you.

Never allow any person to convince you that you're "nothing," and just because someone calls you "stupid" doesn't make it true. Know who you are, and that will change everything.

Because you're a Christian, knowing who you are in Christ is even more compelling. You may not be everything He wants you to be yet, but you're on your way.

In the meantime, walk in freedom, with your newfound knowledge. In this way, knowing that you have needs, you will put to flight *The Enemy Inside Your Mind.*

# CHAPTER 8

# The Battle of My Mind

## *(Or "The Stuff in Between")*

——=➤•◦•◄=——

*For we wrestle not against flesh and blood, but
against principalities, against powers, against the
rulers of the darkness of this world, against spiritual wickedness in high places.*

Ephesians 6:12

I know beyond a shadow of a doubt that I'm saved, and
I'm glad to be saved. I know that it was God's amazing grace that saved me, and I also know that there are
certain benefits that come with being saved.

If I'm saved, I'm supposed to be blessed, because
Jesus came that I might have life and have it *"more
abundantly"* (John 10:10). As a Christian, I expect the

blessings of God to come into my life. However, I have found out that there's a lot of "stuff" in between being saved and going to heaven when I die. We cannot conquer and receive blessing until we have dealt with that "stuff."

Our brave soldiers fighting in Iraq learned very quickly that they could not bring stability to that country until they had dealt with a lot of other related issues, a lot of "stuff." They went into that country assured of victory, but that victory did not come nearly as quickly as they had imagined.

What hinders many people in receiving God's blessings is that they expect to pass over "the stuff in between" and walk right into their blessings. But it just doesn't happen that way. They don't believe that they should have to deal with setbacks, disappointments, the trying of their faith, or any pain and suffering at all. But the Bible never said that life would be without conflict or trouble.

Let's be honest. The Bible clearly tells us that we have an enemy that we must wrestle with. Paul said it this way:

> For we wrestle not against flesh and blood, but against principalities, against powers, against the rulers of the darkness of this world, against spiritual wickedness in high places. Wherefore take unto you the whole armour of God.
>
> Ephesians 6:12-13

We're at war, and we have to face that fact.

I wouldn't want to depress anyone, but each of us must understand that life is a battle. Between being saved and having success and the blessings that God intends for us to have, there's some "stuff in between" that we must deal with, and that "stuff in between" represents the battle of life.

The picture we have of life is often a distorted one. For instance, we often think that other people must not be going through any of the things we're going through. When we look at them, they look so happy and so free. But believe me, if they're human, they go through it too.

*History shows us that we all go through trying times.*

Don't be deceived by looks. Just because someone has a smile on their face that doesn't mean they're not going through some serious trial. History shows us that we all go through trying times.

"They've got it made," we sometimes say of other people. "Their life is easy. Just look at how much money they make, look at where they live, and look at what they drive." Oh, yes? Well, take another look. Rather than envy others and reproach yourself, realize that others have many of the same battles in life as you have (or worse) regardless of their particular station in life.

We generalize, basing the perceived state of a person's life on the things they may have acquired, but they know better. If we could get close enough to that person, more than likely we would be able to see the battle that's going on in their lives. If we could get close enough, we might just learn that the person who appears to have it made actually has to deal with "the stuff in between." This is the warfare that all of us must face.

## *Being Honest About the Battle of Life*

Whether we can get close enough to other people to know the truth about their lives or not, we know the truth about our own lives. We know that we face challenges and conflicts every day, and it doesn't matter how saved and sanctified we are, how big our Bible is, or what church we happen to attend.

We still have to deal with many enemies, so many of them that we must be constantly on guard for them. We live our lives watching for the next attack.

In nature, life can only be maintained at the price of battle, and it's the same with us. Life is a battle.

As we have seen, in writing to the Romans, Paul confessed that every time he tried to do good, evil was present (see Romans 7:21). And he was a righteous and blessed man. Many of us know just what he was talking about. We have been saved, we have Jesus Christ in our lives, and we want to walk in His blessings. And yet we're constantly dealing with "the stuff in between." We just wish that we could move all of that "stuff" that's hindering us out of our way.

"The stuff in between" is always there trying to hinder us from receiving our breakthrough. If we could just get through that "stuff," if we could just trust God to remove it, we could make it in life. We need God. Of that we are sure. And yet, if we're not careful, we can allow "the stuff in between" to hinder us from having the type of communion with Him that He desires.

There may be someone reading this book who has not yet had to deal with "the stuff in between," and you may not, therefore, understand exactly what I'm trying to say here. But if you continue to live, it won't be long before you have such an encounter. Eventually all of us have to deal with this "stuff," because life is a battle.

Think about it for a moment. Whether it's a shrub, a flower, trees, or animals … every living thing survives by fighting for its life, and in this fight, the weakest is crushed and destroyed.

When planning his attack against us, the devil looks for the weakest aspect of our lives. If your temper is your weakest link, then that's where he will attack you. If you struggle with the lust of the flesh or a lying spirit, the devil will attack you in that area. He's always searching for that weak point, so that he can bring you down and utterly destroy you. That's his job, and he does it well.

This same struggle for life is being waged in every arena of life, even in the vegetable kingdom. All of us may know of a garden that was once beautifully cultivated. Because of its beauty, it was a joy to visit. But no sooner was the hand of man withdrawn than the garden became overrun with weeds. Weeds don't waste any time at all. When given the opportunity, they quickly take over.

Even among weeds, there's a constant war going on. One class of weeds will dispossess another class of weeds, until within a few years, successive armies of conquering weeds may occupy a garden.

Wherever there's life, in any form, whether in the vegetable or animal kingdom, there will be a struggle to maintain life. Therefore, we cannot expect to maintain our Christian life and, at the same time, refuse to go through any struggle whatsoever.

We have some serious soldiers over in Iraq right now, and they're not playing games. In order to be effective, they must say, "I'm a soldier. I must remain on guard and be watchful." Here at home, we're in the most serious warfare, a spiritual warfare, and yet far too many of us are playing with the things of God. Too many Christians go to church when they feel like going. During the week, they live any old way they want to live. They give to God whatever they want to give, regardless of what He has required.

These are not serious Christians. They somehow believe that they can maintain a good spiritual lifestyle and go on doing what they want to do. This just shows that they don't understand what life is all about. This is a war that we're in.

It's not easy to tithe when you have bills that need to be paid, and it would be dishonest to act like the devil never tempts us in this way. We try to listen to what God is saying, and yet we have a stack of bills piling up. We know what His Word says, that if we rob Him, we'll be cursed, and if we trust Him and obey, He will open the windows of heaven and pour us out blessings that we won't have room to receive. Still, it's tempting to use His money for our needs.

It's not easy when you have enemies all around you, people who, for some reason, don't like you, and yet God calls on you to continue smiling at them and loving them. His Word teaches us to love even our enemies, to do good to them that hate us, and to pray for those who despitefully use us (see Matthew 5:44). And that's not easy.

It's hard dealing with "the stuff in between." This is the battle of life. If you're like many others, you may be wondering why you have to go through so much "stuff."

You may not understand why you have to endure people who are stabbing you in the back and misusing you. That's not easy for anyone to deal with. Please be encouraged. You are called to go through this "stuff" so that you can receive all that God has for you.

## Progress Comes through Conflict

What is true in nature is equally true of man. All human progress has been made through conflict. Sometimes we can only see the end product of someone who is blessed, but we don't know what that person had to go through to get that blessing. We don't know how much "stuff" they had to endure to get to where they are today. Every life that is built in a godly way must go through some trying times.

Even the intellectual advancement of mankind and the triumph of the human intellect have come through struggle. These victories have been won only after long battles with subtle and powerful foes. Every glorious truth has been won by soldiers of truth, men and women who fought so that truth could be known and understood.

Truth is often not easily understood or accepted. Very often, men hate truth. Some people will hate you because you tell them the truth, but history shows that if you take a stand for truth, you will not be shaken. And, as we have seen over and over again, if you stand on the truth of God's Word, it will make you free.

## Don't Give Up

The devil wants to bring you down with "the stuff in between." You may be experiencing trouble in your marriage, your children may be acting up, or you may have lost your job. All of us have similar "stuff" that we must deal with on a regular basis.

I thank God for all of the many blessings He has given me. Among my greatest blessings are a great family, a great home, a great job, and a great church. I have been so blessed, that for a while, I actually came to believe that everything would be right in my life and that I should expect no worries. God had to remind me that there was still some "stuff" that I would have to deal with.

I have, in no way, been exempt from "the stuff in between." I had to deal with some "stuff," for instance, in the homegoing of my grandbaby. She's not lost; I know where she is; but that was very hard for me. I trusted God, and He brought me through it.

I cannot know what your particular storm is or what you might be facing or about to face, but I would say to you, Be prepared for whatever comes. Go ahead and put on the whole armor of God, and then you'll be ready for battle when it commences.

I cannot know what your "stuff" is, but I'm a living witness that God is able to handle it all. Trust Him. He may not come when you want Him to, but He's always on time.

It may not be a grandbaby for you. It may be some other loss. But no matter what you're facing, know that God is able to see you through it. He can handle your "stuff."

"The stuff in between" can make you cry all night long, but wipe your eyes. You're preparing to come through the storm, for God is able to bring you through it victoriously.

What can you do in the midst of the "stuff"? *Stand.* It may be hard, but stand. Don't give up. You're on the verge of a breakthrough. You're on the verge of a blessing. The "stuff" that you're going through is not more powerful than Jesus is, and today I bind the devil in Jesus' name, and I bind every effort he is making to try to prevent you from receiving God's blessings.

"The stuff in between" will tempt you to miss your destiny. It will tempt you to get mad at God. But don't do that. God is on your side, and He is able to bring you through your "stuff." So don't give up. God can handle your situation.

When you trust God and stand, the "stuff" that was meant to bring you down will have just the opposite effect. It will lift you up. Because of that, I've learned to thank God for "the stuff in between." It has definitely made me stronger.

By knowing the truth about the battle of life, or as I have come to call it, "the stuff in between," you will put to flight *The Enemy Inside Your Mind.*

# CHAPTER 9

# Dealing with Your Enemy

———=»·•·«=———

*Finally, my brethren, be strong in the Lord, and in the power of his might. Put on the whole armour of God, that ye may be able to stand against the wiles of the devil. For we wrestle not against flesh and blood, but against principalities, against powers, against the rulers of the darkness of this world, against spiritual wickedness in high places.*

Ephesians 6:10-12

We're the people of God, but if we are to have victory, we must take authority over the enemy. It is time that we learned the truth about him.

In this passage, the apostle Paul indicates that we are the only ones who can successfully win this battle. This "*we*" referred to in verse twelve is not mankind in general, but the people of God specifically. The world suffers because of the powers of evil, but the child of God can successfully wrestle or contend with those evils.

The people of the world are not generally concerned about wrestling against evil. They have come to accept that the evil that exists in the world is normal. Because of that, they're indifferent to sin and the problems it causes in the world around them. But children of God can never afford to become complacent.

When a child of God sees the evils of the world, they begin to wrestle with the enemy, knowing that they have the authority to cast the devil down. We can actually bind the *"strong man."*

### Binding the Strong Man

Jesus said:

*When a strong man armed keepeth his palace, his goods are in peace: but when a stronger than he shall come upon him, and overcome him, he taketh from him all his armour wherein he trusted, and divideth his spoils. He that is not with me is against me: and he that gathereth not with me scattereth.*

Luke 11:21-23

When we look at this passage of Scripture in context, we notice that Jesus was responding to a challenge presented to Him while He was casting out demons. This was an area of His ministry that was continually questioned by the people of His day, and it is still questioned today by those who approach the Scriptures intellectually.

Far too many people try to figure out God's Word with their minds. They calculate and reason, and when things don't seem to add up in their way of thinking, they invariably begin to question the validity of the Scriptures. But since God doesn't think as we do, this should not surprise us.

God does things the way He wants to do them, and He does them where and when He wants to do them. So stop trying to figure Him out.

The group of people who did not feel comfortable with Jesus casting out devils came to the conclusion that He was doing it because of His relationship to Beelzebub (see Luke 11:14-15). Beelzebub was the prince of demons, Satan himself. So, when the people said this, they were attributing Jesus' power to Satan.

The name Beelzebub literally means "lord of the flies." The Jewish people regarded hell as a cosmic garbage dump, and in a very real sense they were right. Hell is filled with wasted lives. And, because a garbage dump always attracts flies, they called the devil Beelzebub, the lord of the flies.

All of us need to examine ourselves to see who we are attracting and why we are attracting them? Are you attracting flies? Are nosy and gossipy people drawn to you? Are people who lie and cheat drawn to you? Do you have the spirit of Beelzebub? It never hurts to ask yourself these questions, because this kind of spirit is lurking around.

Our elders used to quote the saying, "Birds of a feather flock together." We must be careful to operate in the Spirit, so that we can attract people who do the same.

## Satan's Not Divided

The people who confronted Jesus this particular day were sure that He must have a relationship with the lord of the flies, but Jesus told them that they were wrong. If He had been casting out devils by the power of Beelzebub, Satan's kingdom would be divided against itself. Satan would be pitting himself against the demons under his authority. And Satan never fights himself. He's much too clever for that. He understands that if he fights against himself, his kingdom will fall.

Demonic spirits work together, and they know just what people they should get to cooperate with them. If you're a gossiper, gossiping spirits know just the right people to connect you with, people who will help you cause trouble by gossiping and by listening to gossip. This is the way Satan can build his kingdom.

Meanwhile, God is trying to get His people to be in one accord with His program, but this seems to be a very difficult task. The devil seems to accomplish unity easily, but Christians still struggle with it. What would happen if all the people of God, all those who have professed to join themselves to Him, would suddenly come together and work in unity? What an awesome team that would be!

Wouldn't it be great if all of the church people who love to murmur and complain and concentrate on the bad things going on around them would decide to pull together with us, instead of dividing us further? At some point, the people of God must do just that.

When Jesus said that Satan was too clever to work against himself, He was suggesting that anyone who was under the control of Satan had no hope of deliverance apart from the intervention of an outside force. If someone is bound, there's no way for them to have victory without God's intervention. Nothing else will change their situation.

### At Peace with the "Strong Man"

If we're to get a clear understanding of Luke 11:21-23, we must look at it very carefully.

This text mentions the *"strong man."* Who is he? He's none other than Satan himself. The term "the palace" or *"his palace"* refers to the world and everything that the world has to offer. The goods in the palace, or *"his goods"* simply refer to mankind everywhere.

*When you're in charge of your own house, but you allow Satan to rule in your temple, you're actually putting him in control of your life.*

When you're in charge of your own house, but you allow Satan to rule in your temple, you're actually putting him in control of your life. When this happens, the Bible shows here that you are at *"peace"* with him. You have become his *"goods"* and are allowing your actions to be controlled by him, so you are no longer wrestling against him. And, since the devil is in control of you, he also doesn't have to fight against you. This makes him very happy.

Satan will never tell anyone to stop living in a common-law relationship. Rather, he will say, "That man is taking good care of you, so don't be so foolish as to listen to what your preacher's saying to you. That man has given you your own credit card and your own car, so don't spoil it. If you want to hear what your preacher says, that's fine, but just let it go in one ear and out the other."

Why would Satan want to attack this house? It's already his. *"His goods are in peace."*

When the devil is disturbed by anything, the first thing he cries out is, "Leave us alone." If he's ruling your temple, for example, and you hear a sermon against living in common-law marriage, the first thing you may want to say is, "Pastor, why did you have to bring that up? Why not just preach something positive and leave well enough alone? Why do you always have to meddle in everybody's personal business?"

That's the demon talking. He's saying, "Leave us alone. Why can't we all just get along?" He always gets upset when the Word of God is being taught or preached because he knows that someone is attacking his stronghold.

### *"Leave Us Alone"*

When the devil is in charge of a particular house, he guards it jealously and tries to prevent the Word of God from getting into the hearts of the people who live there. That's why he never wants people to go to church, and he will encourage them to use any excuse whatsoever not to attend.

He convinces many to miss their regular church services on special holidays. He doesn't want them to receive the Word because of its liberating power. If he can keep them from it, he can control them. He has them right where he wants them, and he takes over their lives and reigns over them.

There are many people who like the way they're living, and they don't want anyone to tell them the truth and disturb their peace. If they want to rob God, they believe that's their business. They don't want anyone telling them what to give. They know that the Lord, in His Word, designated that ten percent of our income belongs to Him, but they don't care. Don't try to tell them what to do. They're at peace with the devil, and they don't want anyone to disturb them.

It is the position of the Bible that the world has fallen under the control of Satan, and it's not very hard to see that it's true. This does not mean that Satan has taken control of the trees and the water or the other inanimate things around us, but that he has taken charge of organized human society. He's in control.

The apostle John wrote to the churches:

*And we know that we are of God, and the whole world lieth in wickedness.*

1 John 5:19

The world is under the control of this god with the little g. He is Satan, the devil. That's why it is so difficult for the people of the world to accept a word from the Lord. It's because the devil is ruling their world, and his word is contrary to God's.

That's why, when I preach, I attempt to destroy every satanic stronghold. The world around us has fallen under the control of Satan, and there's no possibility of its deliverance apart from outside intervention. Because Satan is controlling from within, there is no hope of victory from within. It must come from without. That's why I labor to minister God's Word to men and women I come in contact with everywhere.

The only way that someone in satanic bondage can have victory in their lives is through the ministry of God's Word breaking down the strongholds that exist there. If they're at peace with the devil, there is a stronghold operating inside of them. This is the reason that, when they are confronted with their sin, they respond by saying that they like it that way. "Please leave me alone." But if God says that a certain behavior is not right, then it's not right. Take authority over the strongholds in your life.

## In Order to See a Change, We Must Rise Up and Take Authority

All humanistic methods for reforming the evils of society are bound to fail because they never come to grips with the essential problem. They are simply rearrangements of the difficulties, and they leave God out of the process.

Anytime we leave God out of something we're dealing with, instead of making the situation better, we end up jumping from the frying pan into the fire. If we desire to see true deliverance take place in our lives, God must be actively involved in the process.

When we read about the people in our country who get upset because the pledge of allegiance to our flag contains the phrase "one nation under God," we have to ask ourselves the question: if they don't want to be under God, who do they want to be under? We have to be under someone, and we get to choose who it will be. There can never be deliverance in a person's life until that person decides that they will place their lives under the rule of God.

As people of God, we must let others know that they cannot live their lives independent of God and expect to live in victory. We must tell it and tell it some more until we're able to take authority over the enemy in the name of Jesus. We must continue taking authority over the devil until he has no power and no victory in the lives of others.

### Become Strong in the Lord

We cannot become strong unless and until we become strong in the Lord. That's why we Christians need to pray, fast, and read our Bibles more. That's why we must attend church services more regularly. It's only by being strong in the Lord *"and in the power of His might"* that we can overcome everything that has been keeping us bound.

If you have trouble in your home, you need the power of the Holy Ghost to overcome it. Don't curse your spouse out, and expect things to change. Don't try to physically fight it out, and expect something good to come of that. *Be strong in the Lord.* The God we serve is able to pull down every stronghold in your life.

For those who are reading this book, I take authority right now in the name of Jesus over every stronghold that may be trying to keep you bound. Be free in Jesus' name.

I know where my power is, and I know where my victory is. It's in Jesus. And that's where your victory lies as well. Be strong in the Lord and in the power of His might.

The devil had better look out because we're taking authority over him in the name of Jesus. God's Word declares that every knee must bow and every tongue must confess that He is Lord (see Philippians 2:10-11).

### *"Stand"*

The strongholds that have prevented you in the past from having victory may be pulling you down and wearing you out, but that's going to change. When you have done all that you know to do, then *"stand"* (Ephesians 6:13-14).

Don't give up; stand. Don't throw in the towel; stand. Stand, and God will bring you out with victory.

When you put your trust in God, I guarantee that you will come out of whatever you happen to be dealing with. It doesn't matter how strong the enemy's hold on you has been in the past. You're coming out of it by the authority of Jesus Christ.

You have been deputized by Christ Jesus to use the authority of His name. You're the new sheriff in town, and now every crook (every demon) must go because you have been authorized to deal with them. So don't let the devil intimidate you any longer.

You have the full force of heaven behind you, so every time the devil "messes" with you, he's not just "messing" with you; he's "messing" with the force of God's angels. Believe in your authority, and take authority over him in the name of Jesus.

In this way, by knowing the truth about your enemy, you will put to flight *The Enemy Inside Your Mind.*

# CHAPTER 10

# Who Will Control Your Reality?

———※◆※———

*And there was war in heaven: Michael and his angels fought against the dragon; and the dragon fought and his angels, and prevailed not; neither was their place found any more in heaven.*

Revelation 12:7-8

What God is saying to us in this passage of Scripture is so important. Here we see the end result for Satan and his demons: *"Neither was their place found anymore in heaven."*

In spiritual warfare, two opposing forces cannot occupy the same space. One of them has to go, and God's not going anywhere, This war among principalities involves displacement, so Satan could not stay.

When the Bible says, *"neither was their place found any more in heaven,"* it is saying that the devil and his demons didn't belong in heaven anymore. Their place there now belonged to someone else. They had been displaced. When Christ came, He filled all things, including the space once held, or occupied, by Satan.

### What Exactly Is This Battle?

I think that we can all agree on the fact that a serious war is being waged in the spirit realm, but trying to figure out how this war is being waged is rather mind-boggling. How do angels and demons, neither of which can die from wounds, battle each other?

In this war, we never hear of an angel being shot and killed. What kind of war are we dealing with, if physical wounds can't kill those who are engaged in the battle? How does one side win over the other? There has to be a process whereby somebody wins and somebody loses. What is it? Interestingly enough, the winner in this war is the one who's able to control reality.

Right now, wherever you may find yourself, there's a war going on in the spirit realm over and around you. There are angels fighting *for* you and demons fighting *against* you, trying to destroy you. This war is all about who will eventually control your reality.

As we have seen, there's a war going on between the spirit and the mind, and every time you are about to do good, evil is present. You may want to do the right thing, but evil is pressing you on every side. This is the war over who will control your reality.

In this warfare, the presence of God is real, but the presence of Satan is just as real. Light is real to you, but darkness is also real to you. Health is real to you, but sickness is also real to you. Prosperity is real to you, but poverty is also real to you. Thus, the battle is on for who and what will control your reality.

You and I are being confronted with the reality of both good and evil every single day of our lives, and who wins will depend on just whom we permit to become more real to us. Will I allow the spirit of poverty that is constantly attacking me to become more real to me than God's promise of prosperity? Will I allow sickness to become more real to me than God's promise of healing? Will I allow the darkness around me to shut out the Light of my life, or will I allow the Light to prevail?

Who will I allow to be more real to me, God or Satan? One of the two will eventually be the stronger in my life. Which will it be? Will I trust God more, or will I believe Satan's lies? Which one will "scare" me more? Who will control my reality?

### Allowing God to Control Your Reality

Anytime that we allow the Holy Spirit to take authority over our minds, something wonderful happens. The presence of God increases in our lives, and it happens very quickly. The reason is that we have allowed the presence of God to displace Satan's power in us, and Satan's power over us diminishes. So the more of us that we can turn over to the Lord, the more we will have of Him. When there is less of us, God's presence is manifested more strongly in our lives, and the devil has to back off.

*The manner in which we, as individuals, choose to deal with reality plays a great part in establishing the reality of God's kingdom here in the earth.*

The enemy may still want to bother you, but he can't because you've turned everything over to the Lord. So, when you become sold out to God and have surrendered everything to Him, the devil is forced to back off. His influence over you has been displaced.

When this happens, the things that bothered you before will no longer bother you. The devil formerly was able to make you cry, but when the presence of God is in control of you, the evil one can no longer upset and discourage you as he used to. But when the children of God act like wimps and the church becomes passive, or when saints become carnal and allow the flesh to get involved in that which was meant to be spiritual, then the power and influence of demons suddenly increase.

When demons increase their rule, destructive things begin to happen in our lives. Homes break up, crime increases, and poverty prevails. Satan loves it. He's just having a ball. He loves confusion and destruction. In fact, this fulfills his purpose, for, as we saw early in the book, he has come to steal, to kill, and to destroy.

The manner in which we, as individuals, choose to deal with reality plays a great part in establishing the reality of God's kingdom here in the earth. The way we deal with the things that occur in our daily lives will determine who will have authority over us.

Here, there is a kingdom, there is a people, and there is a territory to be ruled. The question is who will rule that kingdom? If God rules, it will be His kingdom, but if Satan is allowed to rule, it will be his kingdom. So, in this war of reality, whom will we allow to reign?

Satan works hard in the spirit realm to corrupt and control the mind of man, and the tools he uses to do this are illusions based on our own carnal desires and fears. If he can frighten us, he has us right where he wants us, and he uses many things to do just that.

Satan loves to play with our minds until we're too frightened to trust God. When we get sick, for example, he tries to frighten us so that we cannot believe God for the healing we need. God has promised us healing, but if Satan can get us to concentrate more on what doctors have said, he can keep us from receiving the promised healing.

God has said that we don't have to be poor. He wants us to prosper and be in health, even as our soul prospers (see 3 John 2). But if we're too frightened to trust God with what we have, Satan can rob us of that promise too. So he magnifies our problems, forcing us to become terribly frightened. And he uses this tactic to control our reality.

In the midst of all these battles, there's something that we must realize. We have someone greater than Satan living on the inside of us. God has so much more power than Satan. All the devil can do is to create illusions. He makes something that's not real at all to look real. He plays tricks on your mind.

Satan loves these mind games, for he's the father of all lies and all deceit. He wants you to believe that the world as it is today is the only world you can ever hope to live in. But when he says that, he's just "messing" with your mind. He wants you to believe that you need to adjust to the present reality, because it's the only reality you'll ever know. Your life is "all messed up," and it will always be "all messed up." But don't fall for it, because it's all a mind game.

The truth is that God is establishing His kingdom right here in this world. And as you turn more of your life over to the Lord, He is establishing His kingdom in you.

### You're Maturing

You are not nearly as quick now to say YES to Satan as before, so you've grown. You're stronger now. You're becoming part of God's kingdom. You're allowing Him to establish His kingdom in you.

Now, as you surrender your life to God, forsaking your own will and desires, your prayer becomes:

*Thy kingdom come. Thy will be done in earth, as it is in heaven.*

Matthew 6:10

You now want God to be in control of your life on earth in the same way that He's in control in heaven. And because you want it, He's doing it. Every single day that passes, He's establishing His kingdom more and more in your heart.

The devil thought he could "mess" with you, but the more he "messes" with you, the stronger you become. He thinks he's bringing you down, but what he doesn't realize is that the trials and problems he brings your way are actually making you stronger. Through them, God is establishing His kingdom within you, and if it continues, ultimately every other reality will submit to and be ruled by God's kingdom reality.

This is what John saw in his revelation:

*And the seventh angel sounded; and there were great voices in heaven, saying, The kingdoms of this world are become the kingdoms of our Lord, and of his Christ; and he shall reign for ever and ever.*

Revelation 11:15

It will happen. The people whom the devil has thought he controlled, rough and tough people, people we have thought would never come to Jesus, will one day go to a church meeting, and something will take hold of them. In this way, God will draw them into His kingdom. God is establishing His kingdom, and the kingdoms of this world will become the kingdoms of our God.

Every time another soul enters the kingdom, we can say, "Another one has bitten the dust." That's one more soul that God has added to His kingdom and delivered from the kingdom of darkness.

The book of Revelation shows us prophetically that in the end every kingdom and every person, no matter how important, will bow their knee to Jesus. And *"every tongue"* will confess that He is Lord (Philippians 2:10).

Some may wonder how I can be so strong in this belief. It's because I have God's Word on it. To anyone not having a relationship with Him, His Word may mean nothing. But to those of us who have a relationship with Him, it means everything.

If you have ever enjoyed a relationship with a person on whom you knew you could depend, you know what I mean. Their word was their bond.

Then there are other people. When they say something, we know that it's not worth anything, for they speak out of both sides of their mouth.

The reason I'm so confident in what I believe about God is because I have a relationship with Him. He has proven himself trustworthy to me, and I've learned that I can stand on His word.

### So What Is Reality?

Jesus said that the words He speaks are *"spirit and life"* (see John 6:63). There's nothing dead about His words; they're real.

When God says something, you can take it to the bank. It will come to pass. All you have to do is stand on it.

You have no reason to doubt God. You can believe Him because His Word is truth, and it is able to become your reality. Nothing that God speaks is a fairy tale, a myth, or a figment of the imagination.

The world defines reality through experiences, but God defines reality by the truths found in His Word. If you have had some bad experiences, you may be tempted to allow those bad experiences to define your reality. You'll be tempted to say something like, "But you don't know what I've been through. I can't trust anyone ever again because I had such bad experiences in the past."

*Learn to depend upon God's Word as your reality.*

If you allow experiences to become your reality, then that is truth for you, and it will control you. Learn to depend upon God's Word as your reality. If not, the devil will keep you bound in the reality of your own experiences, and you'll never achieve the reality of God's Word.

No matter what you've experienced in life, God is able to turn your experiences around and make them work together for your good. You may well have had some bad experiences. We all have. But don't let those bad experiences define either your present or future reality.

You can forget the things of the past. That's what the apostle Paul did. Like everyone else, he had some bad experiences, but he refused to allow those bad experiences to keep him down.

One example is compelling. Every time people would hear Paul peach, they would say, "That's the man who used to kill Christians" (see Acts 9:20-21). That report could have been devastating. Paul had to learn to answer, "Don't worry about my past because I've been changed. I'm forgetting those things which are behind me, and I'm pressing toward the mark of the high calling of God in Christ Jesus (see Philippians 3:13).

"I have a new determination, so please don't use my past to try to bring me back into that old reality. My present reality is that I've turned my life over to Jesus, and regardless of what I used to be, He's able to make me into what He's called me to be."

## Our Greatest Weapon

Our greatest weapon against the enemy is the weapon of God's anointed Word. This was the weapon that Jesus himself used when He was tempted in the wilderness. He had to deal with the reality of the wilderness, and He did it with the reality of God's Word. You're not the only one who's had a wilderness experience. Jesus had one too.

He had fasted for forty days and nights and was hungry and in need of food (see Luke 4:1-3) when Satan came to Him and tempted Him to turn a stone into bread. The reality in that moment was that Jesus was hungry, and He had the power to turn that stone into bread.

Satan had something else entirely in mind. He taunted Jesus, "You claim that You're the Son of God, so why don't You prove it to me?" But Jesus knew that He had nothing to prove to the devil, and He refused to allow anyone but God to direct His actions.

As people of God, we must stop trying to prove who we are to Satan. We don't have to prove anything to him. All we have to do is stand on the Word of our God.

That's exactly what Jesus did. He responded to the devil with the truth of the Word. He didn't come back crying and complaining that He was hungry. Instead, He said:

*Man shall not live by bread alone.*

Luke 4:4

In other words, Jesus was saying, "Get out of my face, Satan. I need more than the "stuff" you can give me. I need something that will last, and you have none of it. What I need is God's Word."

It doesn't matter what you're dealing with in life, you also need to have something that will last. And only God has it.

Through His Word, God is able to break down every stronghold that has been built up in your life over the years.

### Corrupted Minds

What are the strongholds that are holding you back, the lies that the devil has sown into your mind over time? Because you have come to believe them and to stand in expectation of them, they have become your reality.

The devil has corrupted your thought process because that's how he works. He lies to you and tells you that you can't make it. Every time you make an attempt to trust and depend upon the Lord and to step out on faith and give to Him, the devil is there to taunt you. "Don't be a fool," he says. "If you start tithing, you'll end up in the poorhouse."

He tries his best to control us with such lies, and all because he's the father of lies (see John 8:44). That's how Satan keeps us bound.

That's how he keeps us in abusive relationships. He tells some, "It may be true that he's abusing you physically, but you know that you can't get along without him. It's better to take those black eyes and bruises, put a smile on your face, and hold yourself together." What lies!

Satan tries to keep us bound in any way he can by sowing lies into our minds, and Jesus is the only one who can set us free. We must know that whatever situation we find ourselves in, no matter how strong Satan's hold is on us, God is able to see us through. We must believe and stand on His Word.

I believe in the Word of God, and nobody can make me doubt it. I wake up on it, I go to sleep on it, and I live by it in between. The Word of God is my life.

### Taking Authority Over Reality

Jesus has given us power over the devil. He said:

*Behold, I give unto you power to tread on serpents and scorpions, and over all the power of the enemy: and nothing shall by any means hurt you.*

Luke 10:19

When He said this, Jesus wasn't just talking to His disciples. He was also talking to you and me. When the devil is trying to hurt you, you have power to resist him. You can just step on him.

When he sends his lies to attack you, you can say, "Right back at you, devil, because I believe God's Word."

Our problem is that we allow people to scare us too much with threats about the devil's power, when, in actuality, his power is very limited. Some people threaten to use some sort of dust against us to work voodoo on us. But if we believe God's Word, we can tell them to bring on their voodoo dust. Let them work their voodoo all they want. God says that He's given us power to step on serpents and scorpions. Tell every witch and devil what Jesus said in Luke 10:19, and let them know that you're the inheritor of these promises.

*You have power to walk over every enemy, and nothing can, by any means, hurt you.*

You have power to walk over every enemy, and nothing can, by any means, hurt you. You're covered with the blood of Jesus, and you know who you are in God.

Tell the devil, "Okay, take your best shot. God said that no weapon that is formed against me shall prosper (see Isaiah 54:17), and I believe it."

I'm not saying that witchcraft is not real. It is. But we have something more real than witchcraft. I have never claimed that our enemies are not real. They are. But we have a God who is more real than any enemy. Take authority over everything the devil calls reality, all the things that were designed to bring you down, the "stuff" that was meant to make you retreat, and come against it with the Word of God.

Don't let anything make you afraid. Always remember that God has not given us a spirit of fear, but of power, love, and a sound mind (see 2 Timothy 1:7). Just tell the devil to get out of your mind because you have the victory in the name of Jesus.

Personally, I've made up my mind that I will never give up, and don't you give up either. God is even now ready to bring you to the next level in your spiritual life, so this is not the time to be giving up.

### Jesus Has Us Covered

Jesus came to earth to destroy the works of the devil (see 1 John 3:8). In other words, He has us covered. He knows well that the devil is here on earth trying to destroy us. After all, it was God who had Satan evicted from heaven.

Jesus knows what the devil is doing to try to destroy us, but every time the devil shows up, I can hear Jesus saying, "I've got it covered. I have assigned angels to guard you day and night."

Every time you speak faith, you're establishing your freedom as true reality. You have been set free, not because you feel free, but because of your faith. Stop thinking that you're free because you feel free or that you're not free because you don't feel free. There will be days when you won't feel free, but that doesn't change anything. Even when I sometimes don't feel free, I have faith to know that I am free anyway. God has given me this freedom, and no one can take it from me.

You can have this same confidence. As you pray, God is sending the angelic hosts of heaven to fight on your behalf. And there are more fighting on our side than Satan can get together to fight against us.

God has us covered to the point that we can just rest and not worry about the situations we might face. Put your trust in God, keep praying and loving Him, and let Him handle it. Turn your problems and your enemies over to Jesus, and then stop worrying about them.

## Daddy's Home

Sometimes, when I have had to be out of town without my family, they've been awakened in the night by some strange noise. When I'm home, there might be worse noises, but they don't give them a second thought. When Daddy's home, that changes everything.

Our heavenly Daddy is always home. He will fight all of our battles for us, and He's more than able to handle any situation we might face in life.

I know you're dealing with some real issues, and the devil's goal is for those issues to get you down. But I want to take authority right now over those issues and assure you that God is able to bring you deliverance and victory.

No matter how real your particular situation looks, you can cast down every imagination that exalts itself against the knowledge of God. Your situation is not as big as you think it is or as big as it looks at the moment. All you have to do is look to Jesus and realize that He's bigger than any situation.

This is why the psalmist could say that his help came from the Lord which made heaven and earth:

*I will lift up mine eyes unto the hills, from whence cometh my help. My help cometh from the Lord, which made heaven and earth.*

Psalm 121:1-2

Our Lord will be there in the midnight hour, and He'll be there when the storms of life are raging around us. You can count on it. He'll be there.

In my own life, every time I have turned my trouble over to Jesus, He has been right there, and every single time He worked the situation out. Believe that God can handle the issues of your life, and He will not disappoint you.

You might say to me, "Bishop, you just don't know how bad my situation is." Oh, I can imagine. I've had some very tough situations to face in my own life. I know that you're facing "reality," but I know someone who can wipe that reality away and replace it with a glorious reality.

Some of you can now look back upon situations that you were sure would destroy you. When you were going through that particular situation, you thought you might well be in the last days of your life. But look at you now. A year has passed, or maybe two, and you're still here.

You may have lost everything, and nobody wanted to be bothered with you. But you're still here. This should prove to you that God has the power to take authority over the reality of your circumstance and to cause you to experience victory, regardless of how bad things may appear to be. He's ready to do it for you right now. Just believe Him for it. Believe in the promises of His Word, and don't give up!

You're dealing with some issues that seriously threaten your future, but in spite of that fact, this can be your greatest year yet. Just take authority over the enemy, and don't give up until your victory comes. You have power over him.

In this way, by knowing the truth about your reality, you will put to flight *The Enemy Inside Your Mind.*